T0209236

THE
VIEW
OF A
CHRISTIAN

10 Biblical truths of God's view,
to take you from where you
are into the abundant life

Richard Sallis

WESTBOW
P R E S S®
A DIVISION OF THOMAS NELSON
& ZONDERVAN

WestBow Press books may be ordered through booksellers or by contacting:

WestBow Press
A Division of Thomas Nelson & Zondervan
1663 Liberty Drive
Bloomington, IN 47403
www.westbowpress.com
1 (866) 928-1240

ISBN: 978-1-5127-9264-5 (sc)
ISBN: 978-1-5127-9266-9 (hc)
ISBN: 978-1-5127-9265-2 (e)

Library of Congress Control Number: 2017910172

Print information available on the last page.

WestBow Press rev. date: 09/18/2017

Contents

Acknowledgments

To the many authors, acquaintances, editors, and publishers of WestBow Publishing for their patience and unending quest in assisting me in bringing this dream to print and into your hands.

To the people in my life who have allowed me to practice walking the love walk toward them, in fulfilling the commandment of the Lord, by this shall all men know you are my disciples.

Thanks to those of the body of Christ who have laid down the path of love and faith for me and others to follow so we too may accomplish the will of God for our lives.

And last, to the Great I Am, without whom none of this would have been possible. May the words of this book find a home in your heart so you too can come to view yourself as the Lord views you, equipping you to walk in your God-given freedom and be used greatly by him.

To you, Lord, we give all the praise, glory, and honor, believing your grace will bring us all to the place where we view ourselves as you do.

Preface

This book is about the journey that I am still on and concerns the view that I have of myself, believing that it will inspire, encourage, and impart hope to all who read it. I am the fifth of six siblings, the third of the three males. I was considered the runt of the litter; it could rain, and I wouldn't get wet.

I was the last picked for any activities and the first to be picked on, ridiculed, laughed at, and shunned because I was too skinny; I might get hurt, they feared. So one can see that the view I had of myself was not healthy, good, or beneficial, yet surprisingly, it seemed I was not depressed. Hurt, yes, but I took it as the way my life was to be, so I just made the best of it. But deep down I was determined to show them all how wrong they were, and I became more distant and cold because no matter what I did, I could not change their view of me.

The view I had of myself was all after the flesh. I based the view of myself on my appearance. My physical size became the focus of my life. Thus I found myself walking in total agreement with what they believed and viewed of me. Silently, internally, I measured myself by others' perceptions of me, as I tried not to become that which they saw.

We all started out this way, living up to the views of those around us, and it stays with us even into adulthood. The ultimate lie that we came to believe is there was something wrong with us. (Believe me when I say that this is not the truth.) All my life I conditioned, trained, and disciplined to label myself based on the views of how others saw me and what they said about me, along with their attitudes and behaviors toward me.

Their views, words, attitudes, and behavior stuck on me like a stamp on an envelope, which became the perceived reality I embraced about myself, even though deep down inside I knew it was not true. Yet there was nothing I could do about it—I had trapped myself. At this time I did not know that the view I had of myself governed my entire life; everything about my life came from this view. For example, take education: one of the thought processes I developed in life concerning education was that runts can't be smart, so why bother. *I am never going to amount to anything,* I thought. *This is not living; this is just getting by. Just keep a low profile of yourself. Stay in the box others created for you and don't rock the boat.*

We all to some degree have labeled ourselves by the terms, attitudes, mind-sets, and experiences of others and have come to develop those same views about ourselves, even down to how we live on a day-to-day basis. We all have been raised and disciplined to base everything about ourselves on the views we have about ourselves, which are more wrong than right—but rest assured that it's nothing Father God can't change.

Now your experience may not be exactly like mine, but the principle behind it is, and if he can work with me to bring me out, he will do it for you as well because he loves you. How our Father sees us is the way that it is. We say we know we are a spirit-being, but until we embrace this truth as he has embraced us in Christ, we will continue to live life struggling and compromising our true selves. Our enemy wants us to continue this pattern for the rest of our days because he is so afraid of us removing his lies from our heart so the truth of what we are, what we were created to do, and the blessing we can be to the kingdom of God can come to the forefront of our life for all to see, just like Jesus. So when we embrace ourselves as God sees us, our life will become totally different, and the abundant life Jesus said he came to give us will become our right-now way of living.

God had a plan for my life, as he does for all of us; he knew what I needed; and he knew how to get it to me. His priority was to present me with the salvation he provided for all humanity through the Lord Jesus Christ. Thus, on January 17, 1980, at 7:30 p.m., I received Jesus as my personal Savior and Lord, and this is when I entered into his plan for my life. The day you received Jesus as your personal Savior and Lord, you entered into the plan God has for you as well.

Now if you are not his through the new birth, you can be. All you have to do is receive Jesus Christ as your personal Savior and Lord by believing in your heart and confessing with your mouth. Call upon him right now, and he will save you, making you his; and begin your new walk of life with him. Once we are his, he starts us all on this journey of leading us to change the perverted views we have of ourselves into the view of how he sees us, and what a life it is.

One of the primary scriptures that he used to awaken me to being more than I naturally saw is found in 2 Corinthians 5:7, which reads; "For we walk by faith, not by sight." Trust me when I say that I had no clue of what this scripture meant when I started. But over time, by staying with it, the truth about the view of myself was birthed into my heart. Faith knows the reality of God's perception of me, and through faith is the only way I came to embrace God's view concerning myself.

I had no idea that there was more to my life than what I could naturally see. It was a battle, for thoughts would seemingly come from nowhere to contradict the truth—thoughts like, *How could God see me differently than the way I see myself? Doesn't he know? Can't he see all that is wrong with me? What good is my life to him?* And the thoughts would just keep coming to justify my staying where I was.

But the Holy Spirit never gives up, and I am here to tell you that he does have and always will maintain the perfect view of you. Nothing can change this. He did not put us here for such a time as this to live life without him, but with him. He will train, educate, and discipline us to see ourselves as he ordained for us to be in the last Adam.

So dear brothers and sisters, if you are finding issues in your life difficult or trying, if you keep finding yourself going around the same mountain and dealing with the same issues, always getting to a certain point in your life and never getting beyond it, maybe what's holding you back is the view that you have of yourself.

I have come to learn from listening and paying attention to those more spiritually mature than me, to whom I owe many thanks, that what Father God does for one he has done for all, and this includes you and me. No matter the calling, we all are important to him.

So it's time to destroy that perverted view we have of ourselves, arise and take our rightful place in Christ Jesus, and to live life at the level he has ordained for us to live by seeing ourselves the way he sees us. Let's rise up on the inside, draw the line in the sand, and declare, "From this point forward I will not let my heart continue to be troubled any longer. There is a divine hope and a victorious life that awaits me. It's been purchased for me by the blood of Jesus."

If you can identify that the view of yourself needs work, read on, and glean from the words that follow whatever you need to assist you in walking in the light, life, and power of the view God has of you.

It's my prayer that as you continue to read, the Lord will enlighten the eyes of your understanding and cause the light of his truth to dawn upon your heart. He wants you to know that you can change the view of yourself as being a Christian and walk in the freedom and victory he has personally provided for you. Prepare to be lifted up above your enemies, standing in faith, and embracing your God-given destiny as you allow him to change your view of yourself into his view of you so you can live the life destined for his glory.

Chapter 1

Importance of View

Everywhere we look, we are bombarded daily with opinions on how we are to see ourselves and how others see us while also facing an all-out wall-to-wall assortment of media sources. Through advertisements and marketing strategies, they push us to identify ourselves with their products in the hopes of getting us to maintain or develop a certain view of ourselves through purchasing those products. They offer us the promise of a rich, full, and complete life, and to some extent we all bought into it growing up.

The view we have of ourselves began developing when we were young children. We've been disciplined, trained, and schooled to adopt the views of family, friends, and society. The media channels display products for us to desire in the hopes that their products will make us fit in, be accepted, run faster, jump higher, and be better than anyone else, thereby making us the envy of others.

We often find aspects of our personal life and the media working hand in hand, forcing their views upon us in the attempt to mold us into the view they want us to have. The airways are flooded daily with images of all sorts of products—what to eat, what to drink, and what to wear. They work to get us to take in the thought that their products will improve our life. Their goal is to convince us that if we had these products, we would satisfy ourselves and have a richer life than what we have always known, but this is the furthest thing from the truth. Nothing of this physical world can satisfy us like the view God has of us.

Every person has an image within that dictates and governs every aspect of his or her life. Take communicating with other people, for example. The image we have of ourselves determine the interactions we have with them. When I had a low view of myself and someone gave me a compliment, I would outwardly agree, but internally it did not fit with how I saw myself. It was hard for me to be open or be a part of anything wholeheartedly. I filtered the compliment through this inner picture I had, and my internal response was, *You don't know me.* Yes, I would go through the motion of acceptance so as to not offend someone, but the low image of self-rejection, of seeing myself as being unworthy and not measuring up, ruled my thinking.

Nothing we strive for, determine, or refuse to do is done without first looking inside at the view we have of ourselves, to see if we can or should participate. It's this inner view we have by which we judge ourselves. Thus, in people's heart, there are images of how we truly see ourselves, and it's these views that everyone else gets to see through how we live.

The view we have concerning ourselves is important for us to see and understand. It's the major foundation of our very life. Proverbs 23:7 says, "For as he thinketh in his heart, so is he: ...." Our ability to view is a virtue, given to us by God by which we live. Therefore, children of God, we need to see ourselves as God made us to be; we must return to the right image we were created to have. His view of us is the only view of ourselves by which we will live the rich, full life he created us to have.

Jesus put it this way: "I am come that you might have life and have it more abundantly" (John 10:10). My hope for you is that in the following pages you will find the truth to assist you in having peace with God, yourself, and others. Take a moment and ask yourself, *Do I see myself the way Father God sees me?* And if you answer that you don't know because you aren't sure how God sees you, you are in the right place at the right time to step into the abundant life he has for you.

Proverbs 4:7 says, " ..., and with all thy getting get understanding." Defining a word is one of the ways we ensure that we get an understanding and increase the opportunity for us to walk in our freedom.

View is a powerful word. According to *Webster's Revised Unabridged Dictionary 1913 Edition,*[1] *view* as a verb means the following: "the act of seeing or beholding; examine by the eye; inspection. Mental survey, intellectual perception, or examination. Power of seeing, either naturally or mentally, to think of something in a particular way; to look at attentively, to scrutinize, observe, to survey or examine mentally."

Another word with a similar definition *conception*, which means, as it relates to the view we have of ourselves, "that which is conceived; the act, process, or power of conceiving mentally; a mental impression; the formation in the mind of an image, idea, or notion, apprehension."[2]

The view we have of ourselves is a mental image or concept; it's the consciousness, impression, or awareness we have about ourselves. It's the picture we have conceived as an understanding of who we are. It's personal, and it dictates and governs our life.

We have been led to believe that our genders, the people in our life, the environments in which we live, and our experiences run our life, but they are really only tools used to get us to condition, train, and discipline our heart and mind to see ourselves perversely. A view or conception is a spiritual gift, a force given to us by God so we can function, achieve his will, and live the life he destined us to live. The view we are disciplined to is not the view God has of us, but rest assured he's provided the right image for us.

All Christians should address this issue. No one is too young or too old to have his or her self-view shaped in the correct way. This principle is used in marketing everywhere about everything, no matter our age, gender, education, or income. Marketers understand how important the view we have of ourselves is.

They focus on the power of our ability to view ourselves in such a way that we want to buy their products, for they know that if we can see ourselves with them, we will buy them. They work to get us to see the need for their products; they push their products' benefits and tell us how they will improve our life. "Eat this to build stronger muscles." "Wear these shoes to run faster and jump higher." "Take this pill to open up your mind and think like never before." And what about lipstick, clothes, cologne, perfume, vehicles of any type, houses, jobs, the military, or schools? Nothing is off limits. All of these images show what they say we could be if we purchased their products or went to their schools.

Despite all this, the only one who has the perfect view for us is God. He created us with the right view we are to have of ourselves. Genesis 1:26 states that God said, "Let us make man in our image and after our likeness and let them have dominion…" The view that God has of us is the view that we are to have of ourselves. This view is the perfect view—the highest view, the only view by which we will live the rich, full life that God said we could live. This life is based on who he is and not anything of this world like we were led to believe.

The following pages contain the information and instruction on how to return to the view Father God has for us so that we can live life free from the hurts, lies, abuse, limitations, and deceptions of our past. Faith believes what God says in his word. In Genesis 1:26, he gives us three insights of how he sees us.

First is his image. Second is his likeness, and third is our having dominion. These are the components of the perfect view that he has and that we are to develop about ourselves. In John 4:24, Jesus said to the woman at the well, "God is a spirit and they that worship him, shall worship him in spirit and in truth." What God is, then, so are we; thus, if God is a spirit, then we are a spirit too. Being a spirit is the first truth we must embrace concerning ourselves. We are a spirit; we have a soul, and we live inside of a body. When God breathed Adam into the body he had created, he was perfect in every way, and he started out seeing himself and operating just like God said.

But then Adam committed high treason and perverted everything about himself and all of humanity that was in him, waiting to be born. From the fall, he ceased to see life from the spiritual standpoint he was created in and relegated himself and all humanity after him to seeing life only through the senses. From his fall, we were born with his spiritual state of death (separation) from God. Humanity was born with and dominated by a perverted view and perception. From this spiritual state, we could only put natural things first, trusting in any- and everything we could detect with our five senses in an attempt to make our life rich and full, but nothing could.

Our life is to be based on who God is and not the things he created. So through Christ Jesus, we have the God-given right to return to the perfect view and possess the correct perception he created us to have. The view of ourselves is so vitally important to our life; how we see ourselves dictates everything about us—what we say, what we think, and what we do.

We struggle in life because of the view/image we have in our heart. No matter how much we try to change the things in our life, the result is always frustration, despair, hurt, withdrawal, a sense of hopelessness, and nose to the grindstone. We are always pursuing natural things that can never bring us to that place of fulfillment.

From this view of believing we are flesh, our enemy uses every trick he can to keep us from turning back to God. He wants us to keep pursuing physical things such as being in a relationship and education; anything we can see is not off limits to him. None of these things have satisfied us because we are spirit-beings. The devil wants us to operate on our own. He wants us to focus on our behavior, into which we invest time and energy to try and change only to end in frustration, and while frustrated we will give in and quit trying.

We cannot change our spiritual side by natural means; spiritual things can change only through spiritual means. Thus the Word of God is the only spiritual force we have to change everything spiritual about us, restoring our view back to how God sees us, which in turn will allow us to change our behavior.

During a normal school day, a professor set a half-full glass of water in the middle of a table and then asked his students to determine whether it was half full or half empty as they entered the classroom. After each student marked down his or her perception, the professor separated the class into those who saw the glass as half full on one side of the room and those who saw the glass as half empty on the other.

The professor asked students on each side to explain their decisions. After some time of letting them debate their positions, the professor stopped the class and said that no one was wrong; he understood that each person's explanation was based on the view established in his or her heart based on each one's experiences and influences. He said the reason for the glass's status could be known only by the one who had put the water in it and his or her reason for doing so. Likewise, if we are going to understand ourselves, we have to see ourselves through the eyes of him who made us, and not the opinion of others, from whom we did not come.

Seeing ourselves the way God sees us is not going to happen without its challenges. We have an enemy; we see him introduced in the Bible as the serpent, and we know this to be the representation of the devil. In the garden, he got the man to separate from God, who is the source of man's life (Gen. 3). The question becomes how he got Adam to do this, and the answer is that he manipulated the truth to get the man to question his identity with God and ultimately disobey God's will.

Since the fall, he's gotten us to believe that we are flesh and that all we need is something of this physical world to take the place of God in our life. This is not the truth. He gets us to base our view of ourselves on the things of this world. He uses the views of family, friends, coworkers, and the media to get us to keep the view we have been disciplined and trained to believe about ourselves intact.

When man fell in the garden, he died spiritually, and his view of himself changed. Thus, all humans born after him were born of his spiritual state and perverted view. Genesis 5:3 says, "And Adam lived an hundred and thirty years, and begat a son in his own likeness, after his image; and called his name Seth." In separating himself from God, all humanity born after him was born in the likeness and image of his fallen spirit.

However, the view that God has of us has never changed; man

changed the view of himself and, in so doing, had only his senses as his source of life. Genesis 3 says that after Adam's and Eve's natural eyes opened, they saw that they were naked and proceeded to try and cover up their bodies. At this point, man's input into his heart began with his five senses. His view of himself had to change to fit his spiritual state, so through his senses he began to reprogram his soul with this new information of humans being nothing more than flesh.

We inherited this state and perverted view through the mere fact of our being born into this earthly realm. Thus, one of the greatest struggles we will ever face in life is replacing the view we have of ourselves. Have you ever said to yourself, *Who am I? Why am I here? Is this what life is all about?* And what about *I wish I had never been born*, or *What was I thinking, believing this relationship would make me happy?*

We all have heard about and most have experienced what is called peer pressure. *Peer pressure* is the generic term for how the views of others are forced upon us to get us to develop and maintain the view of the first Adam.[3] Don't get me wrong: peer pressure is real. I have been through it. But when you break it down, it's nothing but a scare tactic that's imposed upon us to get us into fear, making a decision that is favorable to others.

Consider this—the intensity of our feelings and emotions concerning the choice presented to us is what gives peer pressure its validity. If we don't say yes and give in, what will they think? Will we be outcast, shunned, treated like we have the plague? Will they hate us? Will we be talked about and ridiculed? The tactics go on and on. Can you see how we have been led to measure our responses by the view we have inside about ourselves?

The battle is not about the people talking to us; the battle is within. Who does not want to be loved and accepted? Who does not want to be a part of the group, included, and seen as a valuable, productive member? We all do, but in this world's system for the child of God, this will not happen.

The view that God has of us is the view we have to re-establish in our heart. This view is consistent with what we truly are in the eyes of God. The day we were born again is the day we were put back on the path to life and to having it more abundantly. Through the new birth, we were instantly made new again spiritually (2 Corinthians 5:17). Our spiritual state was changed from the state of the first Adam to the perfect state of the last Adam. Upon this truth we are to build the perfect image of how God sees us in our heart.

I was born again in a denominational church and, with salvation being the only focus, we were told to hold on and hold out; when we get to heaven, it will all be better. For years, this is how I saw it, never going beyond the books of Matthew, Mark, Luke and John, I was told that the books beyond these are hard to understand and would drive me crazy, mad, and insane.

But the truth of the matter is those books are where we will find how God truly sees us. He does not desire for us to maintain the perverted view of the first Adam. He wants us to walk in the reality of the view in which he sees us in the last Adam, the Lord Jesus Christ himself. Read Romans 5 from verse 12 to the end of the chapter and see the two views that we can have in our heart, which is our life. Take each verse and list each descriptive term for the first and the last Adam side by side, seeing that the first Adam was you before you became born again, and now that you are in the last Adam, you are a spiritually alive being, possessing his life and nature in the eyes of God. As children of God, the view we are to have of ourselves is to be based on the last Adam. The view we have of ourselves determines the type and quality of life we live. This is how important the view we have of ourselves is to be to us.

Chapter 2

God's Unconditional View

The day started out cool but was quickly warming up for the race. All the teams assembled in their groups. The defending champions, who were most favored to win, had been waiting for this day to arrive. Their coach stood up in the midst of them and spoke a word of encouragement before they started the cross-country race. He knew the other teams were gunning for his runners since his team had been identified as the dominant team to win this particular race.

He told them to do their best, don't quit, quickly find their rhythm, and run together. He added, "When you think you cannot take another step, look deep inside yourself and persevere, pushing yourself, knowing that you are not running for yourself but the whole team."

As the race began, everyone was fighting for position. Some of the runners on the favored team got bumped around; some were knocked to the ground and purposely stepped on; and others were elbowed and punched by some of the opposing teams' runners, who had decided to do any- and everything to disrupt the team picked to win.

The favored team members found themselves in disarray. They fell behind the leaders, and before they knew it, the race was over. The runners on the other teams laughed, mocked, put their hands around their throats to signify choking, and generally boasted of their victory over those picked to win the race.

Dejectedly, the runners who had been expected to win walked up to their coach with their heads down and tears in their eyes. With crackly voices, they apologized for not doing better. The coach, being a man of faith, understood that the race was not their life. With a smile on his face, he looked at all of his runners and said, "Pick your heads up. Don't let this experience define you. This race does not change my view of you, and don't let it change your view of yourself."

The runners looked up in shock, and almost in unison they embraced the coach. He had given them a newfound understanding that they had never known before. They saw that the respect he had for them outweighed their performance. The team members looked at one another with great acceptance, nodding as a sign of confirmation. Then the team captain walked into the midst of the squad and led the team in a declaration, saying, "Next time we will do better. We will work harder and keep fighting until we win. We will overcome all adversity. Why?" he shouted. They all replied in loud voices. "Because our coach believes in us, and we believe in ourselves!" They walked off of the field cheering and laughing like they had just won the biggest race of their life, which they had.

The race they had won was inside their heart because of the view and respect of their coach. Our life is not far removed from this illustration. When we started our race of life, we were so excited, on fire, and pumped with enthusiasm. We had expectancy about ourselves. But as we met one challenge after another, our enthusiasm turned to questions. Our fires fizzled, and the excitement turned into discouragement. We struggled, not for the lack of effort but because of a lack of understanding.

As with the runners, when we think we cannot go any further, we must settle our minds, look deep inside, and encourage ourselves to realize that we are not alone. We are a part of the greatest team the world will ever know—the family of God. We are a part of God's team, and quitting is not an option. None of us are to continue to be defined by what we have experienced.

There will be times in our life when we set out to fight the good fight of faith but things outside of our control happen to us, and we don't finish as strongly as when we first started. Jesus said in John 16:33, "These things I have spoken unto you, that in me ye might have peace. In the world ye shall have tribulation: but be of good cheer; I have overcome the world."

Our enemy is the one who trained us to define ourselves by what we do or what we have, but this is not so with God. He defined us according to who he is, and he wants us to understand this truth and to establish the view he has of us in our heart so we can fulfill his will for our life.

The way we address the struggles that we face is based on the view we have of ourselves. If we operate by the right view of being a spirit alive unto God, we will make decisions that are in agreement with his will; however, if we view ourselves as being flesh, we will operate at a disadvantage and find ourselves governed by the struggles that we face as we have always done.

With the wrong view of ourselves, we will continue to define ourselves as being ill-equipped to do anything about our struggles. To run this race, we must have the truth of how the Father sees us established in our heart. He always believes in us and encourages us never to quit, never give up or become disheartened by what we experience.

He knows that the perfect view he has of us will always lead us to overcome in life. He looks to use the struggles of life to strengthen, reveal, and establish his understanding in our heart. So we must remember that our Father is as faithful to us as he was to Jesus when he walked on this earth, and his view of us is not about our performance.

All that we have experienced in our earthly life has been to program us against God. Take love, for instance. We believed that love was conditional, that we had to perform to earn someone's love, and that it had to be qualified for another's perceived love to be shown. But the first time we did not live up to the standard that someone had set for us, or vice versa, that which we called love got cut off until all demands were met.

Our performance is what we were trained to believe in, and it is nothing but a stronghold to keep us from seeing God's unconditional love he has for us. God does not respond to performance; rather, he responds to faith. We must change by faith the view we operate by, changing it from perversion to the one of perfection. He's based his view of us on who he is. He is the Lord that never changes; he is the same yesterday, today, and forever.

If you have ever attended Vacation Bible School, a church service, or some religious gathering, you have probably heard John 3:16, which states, "For God so loved the world, that he gave his only begotten Son, that whosoever believe in him, should not perish, but have everlasting life." Believers know that God's love is unconditional. He loves us because of who he is. His love for us is not about performance, possessions, or position.

People cannot do anything to make God love them more than he already does. His love for us is to be trusted, relied upon, and embraced. He said that while we were sinners, he loved us (Rom. 5:8). His love burned for us even when we were spiritually dead. His love is the love we have been looking for; his love makes all the difference in our life.

When we embrace the love he has bestowed upon us, our view of him and ourselves will be restored. We have been trying to find love and acceptance in all the wrong places, using all kinds of things to try to fill the love void that only God can fill. God's love is unconditional; his love is the greatest experience we can ever have. His love cannot be earned with performance, like religion says. He freely gave us his love, so we can only receive his love by faith (Eph. 2:8–9). We need to press through the limitations of performance religion imposed upon us and by faith receive the truth of all that his love has provided for us.

What I am saying is this: Since he loves us unconditionally, then his view of us is also unconditional. Sometimes the best way to see what a thing is–is to see what it is not. First, *conditional* means that something has to happen first before something else can take place, that an action or outcome is not absolute or guaranteed but is based on certain terms being met.[1] Being raised on this type of love, we have this thinking established in our everyday life. *Unconditional* means without limits, reservations, having no hidden strings attached, being absolute and guaranteed.[2]

From this, we can see why we hold back from having an open heart with him. Through being enslaved to conditions and looking for it everywhere about all things, we look at him that loves and sees us unconditionally with the conditions that we have walked in all our life. It's not that he has imposed conditions upon us—just the opposite. We have imposed the conditions we have learned in this world's system upon him.

The struggles we face in life come down to the view, perception, or image in our heart. Proverbs 23:7 states, "For as he thinketh in his heart, so is he: ...." It's not what we go through that is the issue; rather, it's how we see ourselves that determines the choices we make on any issue of life. In Proverbs 4:23, he says for us to "Keep thy heart with all diligence, for out of it are the issues of life." Our heart is our control center; it's where every decision for our life dwells.

Our heart is where our view of ourselves, our mind, emotions, will, desire, feelings, and soul reside. Our enemy wants us to continue to believe that the struggles we face in life are outside of us, but he is a liar; our life comes from within. The Father wants us to replace the perverted, conditional view of ourselves with the unconditional, perfect view he has freely given us.

God sees the view he has in himself of us. His unconditional view tells us there is nothing we can do to make him change his mind. His view cannot be tarnished by what takes place in our life whether we are the ones doing it or having it done to us. Remember, he chose to see us as he sees us. He based his view of us on himself.

Take this time to make a declaration of faith. Repeat this out loud as your profession of faith: "Father God's view of me is not based on me, my life, or my experiences. His view looks not at the things done to me or the things I did to others. His unconditional view of me is based on who he is, and I choose to repent from living by the perverted view of the first Adam and by faith receive and embrace the perfect unconditional view of my Father, in Jesus's name."

For us to see the unconditional view of God, we are to look at Jesus (Heb. 12:2). Let's look at a view given us concerning Jesus. In Matthew 3:16–17 at the baptism of Jesus. Verse 17 says, "And lo a voice from heaven, saying, 'This is my beloved Son, in whom I am well pleased." The Father was not just pleased; he was well pleased.

Here, Jesus was entering into his earthly ministry, and at this point, he had not performed one miracle or ministered to anyone to have this declaration bestowed upon him. We need to understand this because we have been conditioned to believe that we have to do something to earn God's love. To him, being born again is all it takes.

God is well pleased with each of his children, just as he was with Jesus, and we don't have to do anything. He has done it all. He knew how he saw Jesus, his Son, and he made his declaration of him. According to this scripture, who was Jesus declared to be? He was declared to be God's Son. In Romans 8:14–17, verse 14 says that we are sons of God; verse 15 says that we cry, "Abba Father," declaring that we are sons; verse 16 says we are children of God; and verse 17 says that we are children or heirs—heirs of God and joint-heirs with Christ.

Among other truth revealed here, the Father is telling us his view of us; he sees us as his sons and daughters. We may not have heard him say, "This is my beloved Son in whom I am well pleased," but we have the inner witness of him being well pleased with us. Here we must address a spiritual truth that religion has not given us an understanding about. Genesis 2:7 says, "And the LORD God formed man of the dust of the ground, and breathed into his nostrils the breath of life; and man became a living soul." God knows us better than we know ourselves.

Humans are spirit-beings; we have a soul and live in a body. To

14

become sons and daughters of God, we must be born again, which refers to being born out of spiritual death and being made spiritually alive, unto God. This is what we call being saved. Now being saved is not the end; it is the beginning. Having our control center saved is the next step in being saved.

Some religions base salvation of our souls on works, some base it on God alone, while others don't even address the saving of our souls, rather ascribing to the belief that if we just hold on and hold out, it will all be better when we get to heaven. God wants our soul and our heart saved *now* so they can operate in agreement with our re-created spirit. His view of us is part of our spiritual makeup, and he wants his perfect, unconditional view transferred from our spirit into our control center so that our spirit and heart can operate as one again, the way he ordained for us to live.

This is why he called us to live by faith; we must relearn how to live. We learned with a perverted view to live life from the outside in, basing who we are, what we can do, and how we want to be seen and treated by others on natural things, but now that we are born again, we must live life from the inside out. This is where faith comes in.

By faith, we speak what God says about us. We think the way he thinks, and we act in agreement like it is so. Through faith, we move from conditional speaking, thinking, and behaving to unconditional speaking, thinking, and behaving. Faith is the way we are to embrace his perfect view concerning us. He chose of his own free will the view he destined for us.

Truly, until God, we have never experienced unconditional anything, but it's time for us to rise up and receive the perfect view he has of us. With him we will find all the love and acceptance we are looking for (Ephesians 1:6). Everything we have experienced in life is conditional, but God's love for us is unconditional. His love for us comes without strings and hidden fees that we have to fulfill before he will extend his love unto us.

This world's system is how we have learned to live, falling for every snare and trap we have been trained to submit to, but this world's system does not represent the system by which God created for us to live, and we cannot let this perverted view stop us from living according to his unconditional view that will allow us to live life the way we were created to.

Chapter 3

God's Perfect View

Daily, we stand in front of a mirror of some kind, contemplating what clothes to wear, how to style our hair (if we have the ability), and whether to wear a hat or not. How about our feet—hard-sole shoes, tennis shoes, flats, or none at all? And most importantly, we have to consider the overall color and design of it all to determine if it's all coordinated.

This routine is replayed every day without question because we have been disciplined to think along these lines. All of this thinking is done just for our bodies alone, but each of us is more than a physical body. What we're doing is trying to represent outwardly the view we have of ourselves inwardly.

Some go so far as to change their clothes multiple times, trying different arrangements in an effort to find what they think is the perfect look. Have you ever heard someone say, "Today I feel like dressing this way," and a few seconds later he or she has completely changed his or her mind about that choice for fear of others' comments?

It's not the outer clothes we are truly focused on; it's the view or the image in our heart that we are attempting to satisfy. Our view or image dictates our thinking and determines our behavior. This inner picture governs our entire life. Clothes do not determine the view we have; the view is what we use to determine what we buy and ultimately wear. Clothes are natural items, having no life or purpose on their own; we give them purpose.

Much time is spent searching for the so-called perfect look. We invest energy and money to buy clothes and accessories, thinking that we are dressing our bodies when, truthfully, we are reflecting the image that we have in our heart.

Thus, we need to settle that we are not flesh and that we make decisions based on something other than what we detect with our senses. Buying is an action, not a decision. A decision is an inner thought process we go through to choose or pick things we believe match the view we have of ourselves.

Remember Proverbs 23:7: "For as he thinketh in his heart, so is he: ...." God created us to live from the inside out; however, because of the sin of the first Adam, we have been raised living a life governed by our five senses. The view we have of ourselves of being flesh causes us to put natural things as a priority, always. Galatians 5:16–17 says, "This I say then, Walk in the Spirit, and ye shall not fulfill the lust of the flesh. For the flesh lusteth against the Spirit, and the Spirit against the flesh: and these are contrary the one to the other: so that ye cannot do the things that ye would."

How we walk is important. Here we are encouraged to walk, or to be, what we truly are, a spirit. Notice the two parts of our being in this verse—our spirit and our flesh—and they are at odds with each other. The part not directly mentioned is our control center, the soul, mind, or heart, where the image is the foundation of how we walk.

If we walk from our spirit, we will not fulfill the lust of our flesh; herein is the perversion we have to address. The view we have of ourselves is of being flesh/natural only. This is because we were born spiritually dead, trained to think according to our senses and believing that physical things are the answers to our happiness and fulfillment.

We are not flesh; we are spirit-beings. We have the life and nature of God in our spirit; our flesh is waiting to be redeemed. Both are vying for mastery of our control center. Because of sin, we believed flesh was it, but now we know the truth. We can stay yielded to the perverted view of being flesh or change it and see ourselves as God sees us. Child of God, your quality of life can remain the same or be changed for the better.

Abundant life is the superior life, the highest quality of life God provided for us to have. Thus, we need an image change. The quality of life we live is our choice, and brother or sister, no one can choose it for us. Until we were born again, everything we did originated from the view of being flesh. However, the day we were born again, we were given a new choice—God's choice—to govern our life.

Walking from our spirit is the same as living by faith. We are commanded to live by faith. Romans 1:17 says, "For therein is the righteousness of God revealed from faith to faith, as it is written, the just shall live by faith." Only by faith or living from our spirit will we see the promises of God fulfilled in our life. This makes our heart key, it is the battleground, and it is where the way we live is played out.

Our struggles in life are internal; they take place inside of us, in our heart. The main battle is over our seeing ourselves as being a spirit, like God said we are, or seeing ourselves as being flesh, like the devil has convinced us we are. The one we believe has ruling influence over everything about us, spiritually, mentally, and physically.

The enemy we face does not want us to see ourselves according to the perfect view our Father has of us, for he knows that the day we do, his days of ruling us are over. Let God's view of us be our goal; this is what we are to strive for, never quitting or backing down. He wants us to live the quality of life he promised us.

He wants us to live from our spirit, knowing that we are accepted, loved, and in right standing with him. Knowing he loves us is the foundation to our walking in everything he provided for us in Christ Jesus. He saved us, in terms of our spirit. We are presently being saved, in terms of our heart, mind, and soul (control center), and shortly we will be saved, when we experience the redemption of our physical bodies.

We are in the time of having our control center saved and renewed. The grace of God wants to remove from our control center everything passed down to us from the first Adam because it's a lie. It's all based on our trying to be something we can never be. We are not flesh, rather a spirit-being.

Consider this for a moment—no one is a mistake. God does care. He has given us our potential, our purpose, and our freedom to stop living according to the view of the first Adam, the view of others, the social pressure that the world keeps before our eyes, and most importantly, the perverted view that we were led to have of ourselves. Say this with me: "We are here because God wanted us here. He created us so he could share his love with us and show us how to live supernaturally right here and now."

I remember when he revealed to me that the quality of my life is not in the views of others but in what I believe. He showed me that the view I have of myself governs what I believe, and it did not line up with how the Lord sees me. Life is about seeing ourselves by faith, by what the Word says we are. We must understand some truths about how we operate: what we believe becomes our thinking, what we think forms our view, and this view becomes our life.

The view we have of ourselves came from perverted words and our past experiences because of our spiritual state, which we were programmed to believe; thus, it governs our life. Another truth is that our biological parents supplied our physical body, our house; however, our spirit and soul came from God (Gen. 2:7; Eccs. 11:5).

All of us have a purpose, a plan, and the potential to live life on God's terms. His purpose and plan for us are not for us to just get by. His will for us is to live, thrive, overcome, and be victorious, allowing him to reveal himself to and through us and allowing the supernatural life we live to be beacons of light so others can find their way back to him.

We are more important to God than any other person we know. In John 15:13, Jesus said, "Greater love hath no man than this, that a man lay down his life for his friends." The measure and value of the worth God has placed upon humanity is equal to the blood of Jesus.

At one point in my life, the enemy said to me that if I were not of the fivefold ministry, then I was not important and God did not need me. He used lies to get me to establish and maintain an imperfect view of myself. Can you see how the words I heard repeatedly shaped the view I had of myself, which kept me out of God's will for my life?

Years later God got the truth to me. He gave me another choice to make, a word to believe; he said that all of his children are dear to him. He said the ministry gifts are not to be given precedence over being his child first and foremost. No matter what ministry gift we're called to, for there are more than five, we must settle this truth in our heart: we are children of God, who wants us to become established in our relationship with him.

The Word says, "Can two walk together except they be agreed?" (Amos 3:3). To walk with God, we must come into agreement with his will for us. His view is perfect, his view has never changed, and he has maintained the perfect image of us. When we establish the perfect view God has of us in our heart, we can truly live the life he sees us living.

God's view concerning us is perfect. *Perfect* means complete, with no defects or errors, faultless, without flaws; it is whole, pure, sound, right, and correct.[1] God is perfect, and he based his view of us on who he is. Thus, the image he has of us is perfect. Everything about humanity is founded upon all God is.

He created man to function perfectly like him on the earth. Man was given the perfect spirit and soul and possessed a perfect body filled with life. In man's control center resided the perfect view or image of himself, until he sinned. When the first Adam sinned, his spirit died; it became estranged from God's spirit, and his view of himself became perverted. His body started aging, and from this spiritual state we learned to live life according to our senses.

Therefore, the only input available to him came through his five physical senses. At this point in his life, man lost all contact with him who had imparted unto him his spiritual awareness. The flesh of humans cannot impart any spiritual understanding into their control center; the closest attribute we have to anything spiritual is our emotions and feelings. These two operate back to back—our feelings are for our physical bodies, and our emotions are a part of our control center.

Have you ever touched a hot surface? Your body felt the heat, but your emotional response came from within. What you felt was detected by your physical senses, and how you responded came from your control center. Can you see how your feelings and emotions work together? When we dress our bodies, we feel the clothes upon our skin, but our response to it comes from the emotional view we have concerning the look of the clothes.

We became dependent upon what we learned through our five senses. Think about this: we base 99 percent of our decisions on our feelings and emotions. Why? Because the fleshly or carnal view dominates our control center. Thus God, the only one not touched by sin, set out to free us from what the first Adam subjected us too. (Rom. 5:12-21)

From the spiritual state of separation from God, we see God establish the first of two covenants. The Old Covenant is where men and women were ruled by the senses; they made emotional decisions and operated from the perverted view of being flesh. The New Covenant was established by Jesus; where man is given the right to be made spiritually alive, possessing the life and nature of God and be reconnected to the source of all of the spiritual input they need to live as a spirit.

If you are born again, your spirit has been made new, and God has the perfect view for you to have in your heart. Romans 8:29 says, "For whom he did foreknow, he also did predestinate to be conformed to the image of his Son, that he might be the firstborn among many brethren." The image of Jesus is the image, the view that God has for us to possess in our heart and live life from. He is looking to establish the image of Jesus in our heart spiritually.

Our Father is perfect; there is no darkness in him, nor shadow of turning. His view of us is perfect like he is. He sees us as he sees his Son, praise God. By faith we return to the perfect view he created us to possess. No more judging ourselves according to the things we have or don't have or according to the experiences of our past. We must learn to separate who we are from the things we do. We are not to continue living by the views of others, the world system, or the perverted view we have learned to believe. We are not to let this world's system dictate how we are to see ourselves anymore.

Because we are in the kingdom of God, we have a new view of ourselves. If we take a poor person out of poverty and make him rich, setting him up in a mansion and filling it with everything he could ever need, it will only be a matter of time before the view of being poor would cause him to turn his dwelling place into the view he already has in his heart.

When we were born again, we received the life and nature of God; we were spiritually placed into the position of abundant life and given everything we would ever need. We know that if we die, we will go to heaven, but the struggles of day-to-day living continues. We never touched the perverted view we had in our control center. It is this view that is holding us back spiritually, mentally, physically, socially, and even monetarily.

The view we inherited from the fall of man keeps us from enjoying all the goodness God bestowed upon us. To get to the point where we are enjoying the blessings of God, we have to understand what we are to be doing. In 1 Timothy 6:12, we find, "Fight the good fight of faith, lay hold on eternal life, whereunto thou art also called, and has professed a good profession before many witnesses." We are in a faith fight; this fight is a spiritual one. This fight is over the view or image we have of ourselves.

Remember, if we walk in the spirit, we will not fulfill the lust of our flesh as these oppose each other. The view or image God has of us is the one where our spirit and soul operate in unity. This is when our life will take on a whole new meaning. In fighting, we are determining the view or image we will live life by. The life of Abraham is a good example of how having the view or image of God changes one's life.

Abram was old and childless, but God picked him to bring faith back into the earth realm. Genesis 12:1–3 describes how God gave him the promise of what he would do to him, for him, and through him. God needed faith in the earth to bring his promised redeemer he said he would send. Genesis 17:5 says, "Neither shall thy name any more be called Abram, but thy name shall be Abraham; for a father of many nations have I made thee." Because God changed his name, Abraham had to change his view of himself into the view of how God saw him.

God presented him with his view and thus the changing of his name. By faith he changed the view of himself from being childless to seeing himself as the father of a multitude as God had declared for he was in covenant with God. Abraham embraced God's view, the image he had of him by faith, and the Bible says this about all who are born again. Galatians 3:6–7 says, "Even as Abraham believed God, and it was accounted to him for righteousness. Know ye therefore that they which are of faith, the same are the children of Abraham."

Why is this important for us to understand? Faith comes by hearing and hearing by the word of God. God would not work through the view Abram already lived by; he had to change it so Abram could see himself as God saw him. Abram embraced the name of Abraham, his image was changed, and from this he fulfilled the will of God for his life.

In this, we can see how powerful our view is over the issues of our life. Think about this: if God can do this with a man who is spiritually dead, how much more must he want to do for us whom he made alive unto himself? Think of the possibilities. He placed his view of us in our spirit and instructed us to get it into our heart and soul.

It takes us humbling ourselves to his Word. It's our right to have God's view established in our heart. How he sees us is the key to our victory in life. Proverbs 4:23 says, "Keep your heart with all diligence for out of it are the issues of life." Where do the issues of our life reside? They are in our control center. As we bring our spirit and control center back into agreement, the victory within our spirit will have a way out to change our life in all areas for all things until God's reality of us has covered our entire life.

God has given us the view, the image of his Son, for our heart, which he knows is compatible with the life and nature of our spirit. Salvation is not just about avoiding hell and going to heaven; it is more than just being born again. It covers our heart and our body. He wants to do to our heart what he did to our spirit; this involves restoring his perfect view in it.

So as we stand before our mirrors as we are getting dressed, what we see is not the real us. We are on the inside of these physical bodies. Let's take the time to establish in our heart the perfect view that God has of us as being his children, the image of Jesus, in whom he is well pleased, regardless of the views of others. I believe that hope is rising within you, light is dawning upon the dark places of your heart, peace is surrounding you, and most importantly, an avenue to your heart is being opened to perceive the leading of the Holy Spirit. Believe the Word—you are loved, you have a destiny and a purpose, and his divine power will help you establish God's perfect view in your heart.

Chapter 4

God's Righteous View

On a bright, sunny day, a father and son walked up to the big window of the new hat store called One Size Fits All. As men and women walked by, looking at the variety and assortment of hats through the front window, they noticed hats of various shapes and sizes. They looked up at the store name and then again at the hats inside, and they quickly spoke their disbelief. They could not believe the possibility that one size could fit everyone's head.

Some stated, "I have never heard such a thing," "It's a money-making business," and, "I would never believe there is one hat in the world that could fit every person's head. Just look at the different sizes of our heads."

Most did not enter the store, but a few ventured to step across the threshold of the door and see for themselves if one size would fit all. Some of the onlookers sneered, wagged their heads, and jokingly put down those entering in.

In the crowd, the little boy looked up at his dad, tugged on his shirt sleeve, and with the curiosity of a child, said, "Papa, can one size fit all? Is it possible? Why do they not believe it can be so?" He then asked the most important question to his dad: "Do you believe one size can fit all?" Looking down at his son with as straight a face as possible, the father said, "Well, son, I had never given it any thought before now," as he considered all the hats he had at home.

So they agreed to get some ice cream cones and go sit in the park across the street from the store and watch as those who dared to venture into the store reacted upon coming out with or without a new hat. A short while later, the son, more interested in consuming his ice cream cone than watching the people coming out of the hat store, asked his dad, "So do you believe now that one size can fit all?"

Still looking perplexed, the dad said, "Son, the only way to find out would be to go to the store and try on a hat for ourselves to be sure." Immediately, the little boy wanted to go to the store to see if the sign held any truth. The dad, being cautious, said, "No, not now, son. Let's wait a week before putting ourselves in a position to be taken advantage of. You know you can't be too sure about things like this."

As the week went on, the little boy took notice of his dad changing his hats often for different reasons. Toward the end of the week, the little boy wondered why his dad had to change his hat as often as he did. So he asked his dad about it, and the dad replied, "Son, it's because of how others see me. It's what they believe and expect from me."

The dad held up a baseball cap and said, "My dad likes me in this one. It reminds him of his younger days when he played baseball." The next hat he picked up had the company name he worked for on it, free marketing by his boss to represent his company. The next hat was for his wife, who said it made him look younger when she first met him. He had a hat for those he fished with, played recreational games with, his sports buddies, and even for those who were casual acquaintances.

The dad looked at his son and said, "'One size fits all' is hard for me to believe, for all the hats I have are for the purpose of how certain others view me." Again in a childlike manner, the little boy asked, "Dad, what hat do you have that represents how you view yourself?" Still looking perplexed at his son's curiosity, the dad replied, "Oh, son, I don't have a favorite. Everyone has a hat for me. I spend my time wearing hats that represent the views others have about me and their expectations concerning me."

The last day of the week had come. As the dad sat in his favorite chair, the little boy approached to remind him of the promise to go to the One Size Fits All store; his son, the beginning of another hat.

We too wear hats for all the people in our life. We put on invisible hats according to how others see us, what they think about us, and what they expect from us. All of our life, we have been catering to others' views of us.

We must change this. The only view we should have in our heart is God's view of us. There is only one view that God gave humanity that is the right size for all; this view covers us all in every way. The view God has of us is the right view; it's the only one whereby we can live the full life God has given us to live. The view we presently live by is the direct result of being born spiritually dead: daily we pursued people, places, and things trying to find ourselves, who we are, where we belong, our reason for being, even what we were to become in life.

In this pursuit of belonging, we put on hats for the many people we encountered. From this lifestyle, we found ourselves being all things to all people, basing life on the acceptance of others, and at the end of the day, we had no idea who we were. We learned to base the view we had of ourselves on the views, thoughts, behavior, and expectations of others. We invested time into grouping people into categories for the hats we wore, for simplicity's sake.

Because we are children of God, he expects us to see ourselves as he declared we are. He did not create us to base the view of who we are on anyone but himself. Child of God, one of the worst realities we can face in life is to live not possessing the right view of self, which leads to our not knowing who we truly are.

He specifically created and designed us the way he wanted us to be so we could fulfill his will for our life here on earth. He created us for his purpose and design, so the only one we have to please in life is him. Psalms 139:13–16 says, "For thou hast possessed my reins: thou hast covered me in my mother's womb. I will praise thee; for I am fearfully and wonderfully made: marvelous are thy works; and that my soul knoweth right well. My substance was not hid from thee, when I was made in secret, and curiously wrought in the lowest parts of the earth. Thine eyes did see my substance, yet being unperfect; and in thy book all my members were written, which in continuance were fashioned, when as yet there was none of them."

Here we are told how he made us. All we are (spirit, soul, body) has been of God's will. He goes on to tell us that we are fearfully and wonderfully made. Oh, to see ourselves as he sees us! If anyone knows what we are and how we are to view ourselves, God does, for we are of his purpose and design. We are not just fearfully and wonderfully made; we are also marvelous in his eyes. We are distinguished people in the eyes of God. The days of being governed by those who did not create us are over.

To God, we are marvelous and distinguished people in his eyes. *Marvelous* is an impressive word. *Webster's Unabridged Dictionary 1913 edition + 1828* defines it as follows: "a) to be made different, b) to mark off by some characteristic, c) separated from others by distinct difference; having, or indicating, superiority; eminent or known, d) extraordinary."

God has made us different than others who have not been born again; he has given us his life, his nature; he knows us intimately and made us extraordinary and distinguished people. The Good News Bible (GNB) states in Ephesians 2:10, "God has made us what we are. He has created us in Christ Jesus to live life filled with good works that he has prepared for us to do."

The day we received Jesus as our personal Savior and Lord, we were born again; we entered into being fellow citizens with the saints and are of the household of God. We are a holy temple and are a part of the habitation of God, being his dwelling place upon the earth. God's view of us is the only view fitting all of his children; this one view fits us all. His view is the only one he accepts as being the right view for his family.

In my life as a youngster growing up, the adults of my day would ask me a specific question about myself that portrayed that they knew everything about me they needed to know. The question they asked was, "Who are your people?" They were asking about my parents.

At face value, this sounds like an innocent question, but in reality, it wasn't; it was another hat put on me reflecting the view of others, and they based their like or dislike of me on their acceptance or rejection of my parents.

To them, their knowledge of my parents held all the truth they needed to know about me. Based on the view they had of my parents, they held the same view of me. Based on my answer, they determined if I were good enough to be around and play with their children. This one act (their hat imposed upon me) forced me to see myself wrongly and work to change my life to fit their views in the hopes that they would deem me okay to be around them and play with their children.

Situations like this are how we were led to program our heart to submit to the views others had of us. This is how we learned to live up to others' standards for us so that we would feel like we are okay or acceptable to them. The trap of the enemy is to keep us blinded from seeing that we were programmed by God to be loved and accepted.

Not seeing ourselves in the right light forced us to depend upon the views of others to establish our identity, believing we were getting from them what can only come from God. Ephesians 1:6 says, in part, "We are accepted in the beloved." Man can assist us only in seeing how God sees us; we have to learn to look at the people whom we allow to speak into our life, for not all men have faith, and evil communication corrupts good manners.

We should not look at our past, what people did to us, or the choices we made; we should just look at God's view of us first. With the wrong image, what could we do? We need to get the Bible truth in our heart, such as that God did not put us here to be all things to all people, nor did he put us here to find what we are looking for in others. This privilege he has reserved for himself.

He is the total sum of what we are looking for in life. He created us, he established us, and he took the burden upon himself to sustain us—spirit, soul, and body. We must give the spiritual realities God has given to us in Christ Jesus top priority.

After becoming a child of God, I heard the Lord say to me,

"Until you develop the view I have of you, you will continue to live by the view others have of you." When we live by the view others have of us, we are living to please them. We must believe this truth God has given us to live by, which is that his view of us truly fits all his children.

One size does fit all, praise God. God's view of us fits us all. He sees us all equally, the same, for we were baptized into Christ. The image of Christ is the only view acceptable to God. God desires for us to know and fellowship with him, and to accomplish this he had to re-create us and provide a new image for our heart. In 2 Corinthians 5:21, we find, "For he hath made him to be sin for us, who knew no sin; that we might be made the righteousness of God in him." Jesus became what we were so that we could become what he is—righteous.

The Word plainly states here that we have been made the righteousness of God in Christ Jesus. Notice that with God, we don't have to work to become righteous. In his eyes, we have been made righteous through his righteousness.

When I first saw this truth, I struggled with it because I did not know how to receive it. I didn't know how to work with it, and I sided against it because the lies in my heart about myself were the opposite of this truth. *How can I be righteous?* I thought. *Look at how I live, the attitudes I have, and the things I do.*

In spite of all of the corruption in my heart, the word still spoke truth. I'm righteous not because of what I do; my being righteous is based on who God is and what he has done through Christ Jesus. The view in my heart in its perverted state did not stop the Lord from leading me to this truth. I did not know at this time in my life that my mind needed to be renewed and my soul saved. This perversion caused me to resist the light and freedom in the Word concerning the righteousness God has made me to be in his eyes.

Like Joseph, I went and told others what God had said about me, and just like Joseph's brothers, they were not happy with me because they had not had the revelation I was given. People who do not have the view of God established in their heart will not see, encourage, or be there for you, nor can they support you in your walk of freedom.

Those I shared this truth with were not happy with me because the view (invisible hat) they had and believed about me ruled, which meant they would have to change, to adjust what they expected from me. And in the end, instead of changing, they worked on me to get me to back off of the truth God had given to me.

As you allow the Word to change you, some you know will not be pleased with you changing your view of yourself into the view God has of you. This is a scare tactic of your enemy, the devil, to keep you from stepping into the reality God has for you. Don't be moved by it, but remain faithful to his Word.

We all have based or are basing our life on the views of others to make our life whatever they believe they can get from us. They have views, beliefs, and expectations for others, and when others choose to put those things aside, the fight is on. The devil does not want us to see or view ourselves as God sees us, and he will even use others to do his dirty work. But child of God, rest assured that you are not alone. The greater one is for you, and the anointing is upon you.

We have every right to see ourselves the way God sees us. Make the choice to do it God's way. In every change, a moving takes place, and if people leave you, don't worry about it. You are making a choice that pleases God. You are not responsible for those who leave you. Maybe they should have never been in your life, or it was not the time for them to be there.

We must learn also how to view everything through God's eyes, like Jesus did. Consider Jesus—he knew who he was to his Father, and he never backed down from it, no matter what anyone else thought of him. This tells us that nothing is to be taken personally; people's opinions or views of us are just that—their opinions, their views. We did not come from them; they are not our creator, sustainer, provider, or protector.

I am not saying that people are bad; I am saying that people can be selfish and resistant to change, especially when something or someone they expect to be there moves from that position. God is the only one who loves us unconditionally and accepts us without reservation. He took the right to determine how he wants us to look, and he sees us all the same. If you are a child of God, now is the time to rise up and take your place. You are not a mistake, you are not out of time, you are not born in the wrong body, you are not the wrong color, and you were not born on the wrong side of the tracks. You are wanted, loved, special, important, and accepted. You have a purpose and a destiny; you have been given gifts and talents to show God's goodness to others as you walk with him.

God's righteous view of us will be a radical change in our life. This change is necessary to make our soul or control center just like our spirit. We need an image change, which only God can do for us. We believe and he brings it to pass. He said, in Jeremiah 1:12, "..., I will hasten my word to perform it." And in Mark 9:23, Jesus said, "..., all things are possible to him that believes."

As our view changes from the perverted to the righteous, everything about us will change, and when we look up, the things we used to base our life on, the things we thought we had to have, will have become our stepping stones to the liberty God provided for us. Let me encourage you—your life will cease being a struggle. Rather, it will become an adventure in walking with God.

Start confessing today this simple but powerful truth: "God sees me as he sees Jesus." Begin reading in the New Testament what the Word says we are in, with, by, and through Christ. This is God's righteous view of you. Write down the verses that address God's view and meditate on them, and you also will begin to experience God's reality for yourself.

Chapter 5

God's Established View

We all have to face what we see in the mirror. We believe that what we see is the real deal, the real us, but sadly, it is not. Our awareness of ourselves is based on the view we established in our heart, our soul, our control center. From our control center, we make judgment calls. We judge by the views we established and have been trained to see. The deception is this: what we see is the sum total of all there is.

In sin, we were trained to measure ourselves according to lies, and our enemy used every medium possible to keep his principles of deceit before our eyes. We are far more than what we see with our natural eyes. Even when we look into a mirror, we have this knowing deep in our heart, an inward knowing, saying there is more. There is the cry inside saying, *My life is more than this. There is more to me than what I see.* There are even times when the cry is so painful that it brings us to the point of shedding tears.

In looking in the mirror, seeing our bodies' reflection, we are snapped back to the deceitful reality that if there is more, it's impossible to achieve. Why bother? Nothing is going to change. The sadness of it all sets in, and with a shake of our heads, we walk away, downtrodden and disgusted as what little hope we had drains from our heart, leaving us with the sad feeling that this is all there is.

Child of God, we must believe that there is more to us than what we can naturally see. We must believe that there is more to our life than what we have known; we must keep our hope alive, believing we can find the answer that will put our life on the path of fulfillment, whereby we can come to see our real God-given potential and purpose.

God wants to use our life to make us walking testimonies of his great goodness. He has taken upon himself the total welfare of our overall well-being. Let me say here that God is not the reason our life is where it is. He is not behind the hurt, the frustration, the abuse, the neglect, or the hopelessness. In Psalm 42:5, we are told one of the things we are to say to ourselves. It states, "Why art thou cast down, O my soul? and why art thou disquieted in me? hope thou in God: for I shall yet praise him for the help of his countenance."

This writer knew where the true battle takes place. He understood what he faced. And instead of bowing to the pressure based on what was going on outside of him, letting it rob him of his faith in God, he rose up and spoke to his soul, reminding it of its purpose, which is to maintain its hope in God and praise him while being expectant of his help.

For this writer to do this, he had to develop and establish in his control center the view of how God saw him. In our soul is the view of everything on which we base all we know about ourselves— mind you, without God. As believers, we need to get an accurate understanding of who and what we are. Life is hard when we live on perverted principles from a dead man; we are of the kingdom of God, and he has given us a whole new set of rules to guide our life. In this is the struggle we all face. We are citizens of the kingdom of God, and yet we continue to live by the lies we established upon being spiritually dead in our heart.

Let's say we were raised playing baseball and know the game inside and out. Then we were inducted into playing slow-pitch softball. The physical aspects of the game are similar; however, there are differences where the rules are concerned. So we should set our heart to understand the new rules. It is similar with our Christian life.

We can prosper in life only when we live by the principles God gave us for the abundant life. One of the major rules of being a

Christian is that we must change the view we have of ourselves by the renewing of our minds. To do this, we must re-establish in our control center, developing in it the view God ordained for us, by Jesus. Before we get to the how, we must see the loving view God *established for us.*

How he sees us is like none other. Only those who have established this view in their heart can help us see ourselves the way he sees us. For years, I cried out for more; I stopped believing that by changing my behavior I changed my heart, only to look in the mirror and see what I always saw. I cried out for help, not truly believing God would answer me, which I got from my religious upbringing about being unworthy.

My religious teaching weighed heavily upon me as my cry for help went unanswered. I looked for answers in all the wrong places. I knew the answer existed, but what I did not know held me back from what God had for me. The answer had to come from within me, out of my innermost being. I had to learn to look inside, where the answer I looked for resided. Thank God he got it to me. I could never see his established view of myself by looking to others or this world system.

God's established view is of faith, and we as believers have to establish it through faith. In 2 Corinthians 4:18, the Bible says, "While we look not at the things which are seen, but at the things which are not seen: for the things which are seen, are temporal; but the things which are not seen are eternal." Romans 1:17 states in part, "..., The just shall live by faith." We must believe that we can see things about ourselves that our natural eyes cannot see. There are parts of us that we can only see by faith. This is the real us.

Faith makes visible to us everything our natural eyes are incapable of seeing. We can see God's established view of us. Faith sees only his view. In 2 Corinthians 5:7, we find, "For we walk by faith, not by sight." At this point, you may say, "Well, that is all fine and dandy, but you don't know where I am. I feel hopeless. You don't know what I have been through—the abuse, the neglect, the torment, and the torture I've experienced. It just sounds too good to be true." My answer is, "Yes, I understand."

I have been used to help others in life, and I have never downplayed or treated the issues they have experienced as anything less than vitally important. I believe anyone can be made whole, set free, and healed from all he or she has experienced. Jesus is here to save his people from their sins (Matthew 1:21). Notice that *sins* is plural, implying they are part of a lifestyle; this comes after being born again from the sinful nature of the first Adam. God knows what he is doing. It's man who complicate the plans of God.

For example, being born again is instantaneous; however, being saved from our sins is a process. There were many times I wished I had a quick turnaround, but no, I had to go through the process. And going through the process is where 1) I intimately found out things about Father God that no other method could produce; 2) he walked me out of fear and into faith, and 3) he healed me from the wounds of my past. Every wound that heals leaves a scar, which we are to use to remind ourselves of the victory Jesus won for us.

No matter the issues we face or the areas of our life those issues represent, how we see ourselves is the foundation of the issues of life. Our life is fixable. God has invested stock in each and every one of us. He knows where we are, he knows where we need to be, and he knows how to get us there. The question we must ask ourselves is, *Am I willing to put my life into his hands and trust him?* Are we willing to draw a line in the sand, arise on the inside as his son or daughter, and declare, *No more!* Our days of carrying hurt, shame, and guilt are over! There will be no more looking down at ourselves like we have no worth or value for we will draw our strength from the worth and value God has for us. Can you give God a hallelujah!

Hebrews 11:1 states, "Now faith is the substance of things hoped for, the evidence of things not seen." We have hope, hope is for faith, and by faith we believe God, allowing him to remove from our heart the lies we were spiritually born with. We can live by faith and not by sight. Sight is one of our senses, and our senses are for our body, from which we learned how to see ourselves. We judged ourselves by the natural things in our life and the world; the Word calls this being sense ruled.

Our senses cannot reveal who and what we were created to be. We were created to live by faith. Only by faith can we walk in God's will for our life. Faith sets us on a new path with a new purpose and destiny for our life. God's established view of us is based on his beloved Son, the Lord Jesus Christ. In the Bible, especially in the New Testament, we see phrases like *in him, by him, with him, through him, of him, of whom,* and so on as they relate to us and God's established view of us.

Romans 8:17(a) says, "And if children, then heirs; heirs of God, and joint-heirs with Christ …" God's view of us is exactly how he sees Christ. He made us to be spiritually exactly like Jesus; we are made in his image and are of his likeness. Every part of us is going to be made to look just like Jesus. Being made like Jesus is God's answer to the perverted view we inherited from the first Adam. He chose for us to be like Jesus; now it's up to us to believe we are.

Romans 8:29 states, "For whom he did foreknow, he also did predestinate to be conformed to the image of his Son, that he might be the firstborn among many brethren." In other words, God predetermined that everyone who received Christ would be conformed to the image of his Son. Since God predetermined or predestined us to be conformed, he established the image for us before we knew we needed his image.

Let's take a minute to address another lie of the devil. The above verse refers to those who God "foreknew," meaning "to know beforehand," but this does not mean he chose who would be born again and who wouldn't. For all who choose to receive Jesus as their personal Savior and Lord, he would go to work removing the perverted images of their heart and reshaping it into the perfect image of the one who gave his life for them, Jesus. In 2 Corinthians 3:18, the Bible says, "But we all, with open face beholding as in a glass the glory of the Lord, are changed into the same image from glory to glory, even as by the Spirit of the Lord." This word *glass*[1] literally means "mirror." We should be looking into a spiritual mirror to see the real us. We need to ask ourselves, *What do I see in a mirror?* Yes, we see our reflection.

Notice, though, that in this mirror, we do not see our reflection; we see the reflection of the glory of the Lord. Take note of what he says: "As we see, focus on the reflection of the glory of the Lord as in a mirror; we are changed into the very image of Jesus from glory to glory, even as by the Spirit of the Lord." This is the image we are to return to living by; this is the established image of which we can truly represent God, here on the earth, living the life we were destined to live.

Have you ever read what Jesus said about himself in talking to his disciples? He said, "If you have seen me, you have seen my Father" (John 14:9). The Word also says in Hebrews 1:3 that Jesus is the express image of his person. This is what our enemy does not want us to get a hold of; he strives to make us stay blinded to the reality of how we truly are in the eyes of God. We are told that the only way we can see who we truly are is to look at the glory of the Lord.

Okay, how do we do this? This is not a one-answer question. The first answer is faith. We have to leave the realm of our senses. We have to retrain our feelings and emotions to follow our spiritual lead. This entails agreeing with God regardless of whether what we naturally see is in line with the Word or not, and we will come to see over time of being faithful that all natural things will come into agreement with the Word. The second answer is the Word (James 1:21–25). James 1:25 states, "But whoso looketh into the perfect law of liberty, and continueth therein, he being not a forgetful hearer, but a doer of the work, this man shall be blessed in his deed." To see the real us, we have to not only know the Word; we must become intimate with it.

God's plan is to change us from the inside out. As he changes our image, we will come to see that the view we have of ourselves will also change. God's established view of us is based on Jesus. Being a Christian is more than just being saved and avoiding hell. It is living the life of Christ Jesus. God established the view for us, and we are to make this view the foundation of our life. This established view of God cannot be found in our world system, it cannot come from other people, nor can we create it with our ability. It can only be received and lived by faith in what God says in his Word.

Every one of God's children has one image to live by, as opposed to how we were raised in our biological family, where we found respect of person, favoritism, earn by works, proving our loyalty and maybe we will be treated as members of the family. It is not so with God; the love for one is the same love for all, the place for one is the same place for all, and the position of one is the same position for all.

We must believe that his will is within our reach. In Christ he provided all we need to accomplish fulfilling his will for our life. This truth is totally opposite of how we were taught in this world's system of earning everything. Thus the only way for us to have what he has provided for us is to believe and receive it. To do what each of us are gifted to do, we must release ourselves from the perverted view that sin and life have imposed upon us, receiving and embracing the view God established for us.

We are to go forth in life, not seeing ourselves as a challenger, rather from the position of being a champion, an overcomer, through the established view God set forth in Christ. No more measuring ourselves by all things and all people. No more hanging on to the perverted image of the first Adam and the perverted view of being nothing more than what we see in our natural mirror and all its hopelessness.

We must believe on the inside that we have the drive, the fortitude, and the resolve to be all we were created to be. We must receive God's established view of us in our heart. What is the drive in you to do? What do you see yourself accomplishing in life? What do you see others struggling with that generates inside of you an excitement, a knowing, a desire to get in there and help?

This is your passion, and when it is coupled with the view established for you, your desire will rise up within you, propelling you into God's plan for your life. God's view of us is a view with a purpose. It is a view representing the problem solving, the caring heart, and the blessing bestowing ability of God. The view he established for us is the view of a champion, an overcomer. Don't be concerned about others' not understanding you. Remain true to the will of God and the view he has of you, and let him transform your life into all he says it is to be.

To God there is no other being on the face of this planet exactly like another. Living up to the potential all of us inherently has requires each of us to develop the view God established for us, whereby we can use our talents, abilities, and strengths to be the blessing he created us to be. The contentment we look for will never come from outside of us; the acceptance we have been looking for will only come from within our heart.

When we live by God's view of us is when we walk in our destiny. We can only know how truly happy we can be when we are living according to God's view. We truly know that physical things, people, and even money fall short of satisfying us. These things are a trap, a temporary, deceptive fix which fails to bring any kind of peace God says we are to have.

We are spirit-beings; we need the spiritual answers God has provided for us so we can go about the life he prepared for us to live. In closing out this chapter of God's established view, think for a moment of how you view yourself. Write some of those terms, names, or phrases down; get them out on paper and look at them.

What you listed has never been nor ever will be the view God has of you. They can be changed. God's established view of you will eradicate the image of these things as he establishes his view in you. But you have made a quality decision to break free and step over into the victory and freedom God has waiting for you. Here is a taste of God's established view of us. Some of the descriptive terms he uses to express his view of us is a view of our being of royal heritage—honorable, righteous, respectful, glorious, just, whole, rich, powerful, and anointed.

For every ungodly name we labeled ourselves with, the truth of how we really are was established first by God. For the view of being a pauper, our original view was of being a prince; for the view of being a beggar, the original view is of us being rich; for the view of being unrighteous, the original view is of us being righteous; for unholy, holy; for weakness, strength; for rejection, acceptance; for sorrow, joy. I hope you can see the difference in how the world sees you, which is based on flesh and your performance, and how God truly sees you, based on who he is, all he has provided, and the view he has established for you in Christ.

It's time to say what the Word says about us. We are not what we have been led to believe, we are not how people treated us, we are not the experiences we have lived through, and we are not the lies we have spoken over ourselves, nor the lies of others. We are exactly how God made us to be. We are just like Jesus in his eyes. Take a step of faith into God's original design. Walk in the view your heavenly Father established for you.

Chapter 6

God's Heavenly View

God's view of us is nothing like the view we inherited from the first Adam. His view is not an earthly one; it is heavenly and God ordained, and he is waiting to manifest it unto all of his children. In the world we live in, religion has gotten us to try to mix the two views into one. We call this a hybrid. *Hybrid,* according to *Merriam Webster's Online Dictionary*, means "of mixed origin; a person whose background is a blend of two diverse cultures or traditions; crossbreeding; a mixture of different things or styles."[1]

A hybrid is not pure; it's the mixture of two separate things, often in the hopes of making something as good as what already is pure. God's view of life and the perverted view of the first Adam cannot be mixed; this is why he provided salvation for us. He established the means whereby we could have his view of us.

God's will is that we not attempt to mix the two views; rather, he wants us to completely change the view in our heart. The Word tells us of the two Adams—the first Adam whom we know from Genesis, and the last Adam whom is the Lord Jesus Christ. We can put it this way: the first Adam represents the earthly view after the fall and last Adam represents the heavenly view by the new birth.

In the world, we learned how to base our life only on the things of this world in an attempt to have a perfect life. In religious churches, it's a belief based on works, on what we can do to earn our way, with no faith in what God provided for us. We can't earn anything from God; he tells us to believe we receive. We see this principle in operation when, on church days, we see what appears to be the heavenly view, and on other days, we see the earthly view.

Have you ever heard people say they were Christians, declaring that they're carrying the heavenly view, and then one day you saw them behave selfishly and pridefully, not representing God? They act like there isn't anything heavenly about themselves. Not to judge anyone, but this hybrid life leads to confusion, and our enemy will use that confusion to play mind games with us.

The hybrid life occurs when one attempts to mix earthly and heavenly principles into one. This is not the life he called us to live. Although we are in the world, we are not to continue to act as though we are of it. John 17:14–16 says, "I have given them thy word; and the world hath hated them, because they are not of the world, even as I am not of the world. I pray not that thou shouldest take them out of the world, but that thou shouldest keep them from the evil. They are not of the world, even as I am not of the world." Twice, Jesus said that we are not of the world, and he asked his Father not to take us out of the world but to keep, protect, and guard us, watching out for our well-being while we are in this world.

Another term used to describe being saved or born again is to be birthed from heaven. We were born again from the power of the kingdom of God. By birth, we are born out of this present world and birthed (spiritually) from the realm of heaven. Remember the story in John 3, when Jesus talked with Nicodemus concerning being born again. Man is a spirit and must be born again. Jesus died for all humanity to be birthed out of death and into the life and nature of God, being made citizens of heaven.

Humanity is to experience two births. We know of the natural birth. The spiritual birth, or heavenly birth, is where a person receives Jesus as his or her personal Savior and Lord and is birthed anew, born from above, possessing the life and nature of God. Everyone who's received Jesus has experienced the heavenly birth. You are born from above; you now possess the life and nature of God, spiritually.

We need to take this reality and create the view of it in our heart. (For those who haven't yet received Jesus, now is your time to let him take you out of the family of darkness and be born into the family of God.) Romans 10:13 declares, "For whosoever shall call upon the name of the Lord shall be saved." This is the beginning of your new life in Christ.

In being born again, the only change we experience was spiritual; our heart and body remained the same. We still have the same thoughts, desires, will, imaginations, and emotions, and our physical appetites and behaviors continue like nothing has happened. In being born again, we become positioned to develop God's heavenly view of ourselves in our heart. He desires for us to see ourselves as he sees us, which makes all the difference while we are here in this world.

Pay attention to these next words—we can't believe something that we don't know exists or that we think we don't have a right to. You have every right, by the blood of Jesus, to have the heavenly view of God established in your heart. Through his view of us, even though we are in the world, we can live life not dependent upon it as if we are still in bondage to it (John 17:14–16).

With the heavenly view of God ruling in our heart, we then will live a life dependent upon him alone. We can and are expected by God to get to this place in our life, this place of living like Jesus did. Jesus lived knowing who he was and how he was seen by his Father. Therefore, it is imperative for us to develop the same heavenly view of ourselves.

While you are here, say this: "I believe I have the blood-bought right to have heaven's view of myself in my heart, for you created me to exist in your class of being." We are a spirit, as God is a spirit. Jesus said in John 4:24, "God is a Spirit: and they that worship him must worship him in spirit and in truth." First, we are a spirit—second, we have a soul and third, we live inside a body (1 Thess. 5:23).

Our spirit is the highest, most dominant part of our being. By our spirit, we are to rule over our soul; our soul is our servant, and we live inside a body, which is the lowest part of our being. When God made man, man's entire being was correctly aligned. Man's spirit ruled over his soul, and through his soul, he dominated his body and kept it in check. After he sinned, he died spiritually, so his soul then turned to his body and his senses for input.

His body and its senses became his dominant source of information. From the state of being spiritually dead, man lost the right to everything God declared for him to have. All humanity was born blind to the things of God, and everyone after Adam structured his or her life on any- and everything that could be detected through the physical senses. Man possessed no knowledge of the spiritual realm; God's love; or his desire to be with, provide, and protect him.

There came a time in man's life when the heavenly image that once dominated in man's heart was perverted into the earthly view that rules in the here and now. Through this image, we learned to judge, view, and respond, being dictated by the course of this world. We constantly measured ourselves by people and natural things, comparing and competing with the world's view of all humans.

We became slaves to everything the world pushed our way. What is important for us to see here is this truth: we all are a spirit. We are the ones God made legal here on this planet. God gave dominion only to spirits who have physical bodies. We determine whether all the other existing spirits can operate legally in the earth. With the wrong view of ourselves of being flesh or earthly, we allow our enemy to remain legal through our life and upon the earth.

The devil is not God. He is not all powerful, omniscient, or omnipresent. He portrays himself as such, but he is a liar. He needs us to maintain the earthly view of ourselves, thus giving him the legal right to use our bodies, by which he gets to declare himself legal upon the earth and free to do all he wants as he maintains his legal rule over our heart through deception and lies. We can clearly see the disadvantage we keep ourselves in by maintaining an earthly view of ourselves.

The issues we face are not about anything we see. They are about what we believe in our heart. We live from the inside out; thus as long as we believe in our heart that we are flesh, we will continue to be dictated by the natural things of this world. But God has given us a day of redemption, a day of liberation, a day of victory. He desires for us to understand who we are, how we operate, what we are truly up against, and how to get the victory we have in Jesus.

We are a spirit, we have a soul, and we live inside a body. We live by faith. What we need to understand is how we live from the view or image in our heart. Our environment is not where our successes or failures exist; it is where what is internal in us is manifested from our heart. We have been trained to fight externally and leave the internal issues of our heart alone. This we have to change.

We must renew our thinking to believe that everything natural has a spiritual base that we have established in our heart. Being raised with an earthly view resulted in what we believed we are, but once we received Jesus, he made the spiritual us, the real us, new. How does this fit in with the world? you may be asking. We are up against what and how we believe. This involves our words; what and how we think; and the perception, image, and view we've established in our heart.

What we face is what we have been trained to believe is normal. Galatians 5:16–17 says, "This I say then, Walk in the Spirit, and ye shall not fulfill the lust of the flesh. For the flesh lusteth against the Spirit, and the Spirit against the flesh: and these are contrary the one to the other: so that ye cannot do the things that ye would." Remember that *spirit* means "heavenly view" and *flesh* means "earthly view" in the context we are using here. In 1 Timothy 6:12, we read, "Fight the good fight of faith, lay hold on eternal life, whereunto we are called." We are in a faith fight. This is our battle. It's internal—it's in our heart, our control center. The battle is over which view we allow to rule, reign, and dictate our life.

Fleshly, natural, or earthy are the things we have been led to believe are our norm. God did not create things for us to base our life on; he created them for our enjoyment. Being born with the wrong view of ourselves caused us to place a high value on natural things, and eventually we based our life on them. Have you ever noticed your attitude or emotional state rise and drop as the things you have in life came and went?

47

What we detect with our senses comes from a spiritual source. God, who is a spirit, said, "Let there be …," and everything he declared came into physical existence. Since we are in God's class of being, we live from the inside out. This makes understanding faith vitally important. Our physical body is not the real us; it is simply our house. Our heart is our control center, where the views we have of ourselves reside. The view in our heart of being flesh drove us to put a premium on things of this world.

Our enemy uses natural things to distract us, to keep the perverted view of ourselves established in our heart. Things such as a broken heart, unfulfilled dreams, dashed hopes, abuse, poverty, depression, sickness, lying, deceit, lust, sex, partying, drinking, drugs, pride, relationships (evil communication corrupts good manners), and the like are the norm of life.

Norm means "something that is usual or expected; an average standard or level; a rule or authoritative standard; a model." From this word we get the word *normal*, which means, "what and how we expect it to be." Someone who is "normal" is like most people in the way that he or she thinks, behaves, or lives. It means according to an established norm, rule, or principle.[2]

The things we have accepted as being the norm are used to get us to keep our noses to the grindstone and keep believing we are flesh. Being bitter and jealous and having an unforgiving heart and resentment are what we have been led to believe is our norm. Our enemy works against us, pressuring us to continue living life the way we have always known and to believe that what we have always expected in life is all there is.

The world does not like us to rock its way of living. We are the children of light. They who have not been born again are the children of darkness. We are motivated by the Spirit of God and they by demonic spirits. What is normal for them used to be normal for us, but now, because we are children of God, his way is to be our new norm. If the world rejects us, it's because it rejected Jesus first. There is nothing wrong with us; we are under construction, a work in progress, growing in the love and grace of our Father God.

no smiling, happiness, or excitement? The only answer could be that they did not have inner views of themselves of what they could look like. The images they had were not conducive to what could be.

Without an inner image of what we could be, we will put forth no effort to achieve it. So too is it with the things of God. Without developing the heavenly view he has of us—our end goal, what we are to be—we will not put forth what is required to obtain and live in it.

The view we were born with is anti-godly. We cannot hold onto it because it has nothing of God connected to it. In 2 Corinthians 10:5, we read, "Casting down imaginations, and every high thing that exalteth itself against the knowledge of God, and bringing into captivity every thought to the obedience of Christ." Here is our battle.

The imaginations, high things, and thoughts we are told to cast down and bring captive are things we inherited from the first Adam. These godless attributes and virtues keep us fleshly minded and earthly in our thinking, where the perverted view of ourselves resides. There is no life in this view to provide us with the inherent drive that will cause us to reach for the abundant life God has given us in Christ.

Hebrews 3:1 says "Wherefore, holy brethren, partakers of the heavenly calling, consider the Apostle and High Priest of our profession, Christ Jesus." Among other truths in this verse, we are partakers of the heavenly, high, above calling, the invitation of God. He would not call us with a heavenly calling and not have a heavenly view to go with it. He has made provisions for everything we need to be successful in living the life he established for us to live. We must humble ourselves, believing that life is not about us but rather about him.

This verse also tells us to consider and set our focus on the Apostle and High Priest of our profession, Christ Jesus. Hebrews 12:2 says in part, "Looking unto Jesus, the author and finisher of our faith …" One of our hardest challenges is in putting our focus on Jesus. The lie says that if we focus on someone other than ourselves, we are of less importance. The truth is this: only by looking at Jesus can we come to find our true importance. Looking at Jesus is looking in a mirror whereby we can see the true reflection of how God sees us. Child of God, you have every right to allow the heavenly view of God to be established in your life. Let no one or nothing stop you from fulfilling your God-given destiny. Value what God says about you more than anyone else. Learn to view yourself as he views you, and watch him turn your heart into the very likeness of the Lord Jesus Christ.

Chapter 7

The View of Being a Citizen

> I pledge allegiance to the flag
> of the United States of America
> and to the Republic for which it stands.
> One nation under God, indivisible
> with liberty and justice for all.

As citizens of the United States, we stood up every day in grade school with our hands over our heart and recited the Pledge of Allegiance before starting the day's activities. We did this because we were citizens, and declaring our citizenship of the American society at that time was vitally important. We also have a spiritual citizenship, one we have to come to embrace with all of our heart. God has given every person the right through the blood of Jesus to become a citizen of heaven.

In this world, billions of people living on various continents were naturally born on them or have become naturalized citizens of their countries. Without going deeply into the legal processes of becoming a citizen in the United States, there are a few ways to go about doing so.

First, the easiest way is to be naturally born in this country. Second, one of the parents has to be a resident or citizen of the United States; third, a child can be adopted by US citizens; and fourth, one can go through the naturalization process. Once completed, naturalization entitles the new citizen to all the rights and responsibilities of a natural-born American citizen.

Let's look at some of the terms connected to citizenship. Passports allow people to travel to other countries without being citizens of those countries. The visitors have limited rights, but they do not hold the full weight and responsibilities of a true citizen. However, the laws of those countries are imposed to their fullest measure if the visitors break the law.

We also have people called immigrants. These people are citizens of one country who migrate from their home countries to another in hopes of becoming permanent residents or citizens of that country. Refugees are people who flee their countries in times of natural disaster, war, or some other kind of unrest. They are not looking to become residents of another country, necessarily. They could choose to, but they generally prefer to return to their native countries when the threat is over. Many of them risk their lives in leaving their home countries to find a better or safer life in another. With these realities comes the use of green cards, visas, work permits, and other documents that are used to designate the length of time that the immigrants, refugees, or people seeking temporary citizenship may stay in the country.

Being a citizen is vital to our identity as a people and a nation. Merriam-Webster's Online Dictionary, 4th Edition, says this concerning the word *citizen:* "A citizen is a person who legally belongs to a country with the rights and protection of that country; a person who lives in a particular place; an inhabitant of a city or town; especially one entitled to the rights and privileges of a freeman; a member of a state, a native or naturalized person who owes allegiance to a government and is entitled to protection from it."[1]

The world has operated this way for years. The authority given to man upon the earth was to represent or reflect the unseen citizenship and rulership of the kingdom of heaven over his life. God created man to be citizens of heaven; he did not create them to be outside his rulership or governing body here on earth.

God sees all who are born again as citizens of heaven. All men have the legal right by the blood of Jesus to experience being born again. This spiritual birth involves being born out of being spiritually dead and into being alive unto God. This birth gives man the inward reality of being a citizen of heaven. We must come to realize this simple truth: our true citizenship is a spiritually based reality to which we must yield by faith. Spiritually, we are talking about a position in the kingdom of heaven.

John the Baptist came preaching, "..., Repent ye: for the kingdom of heaven is at hand" (Matt. 3:2). When the disciples asked Jesus to teach them to pray, part of the prayer he taught them made reference to the kingdom reality of God: "Thy Kingdom come. Thy will be done in earth, as it is in heaven" (Matt. 6:10). In the New Testament, we see references to the kingdom of heaven and the kingdom of God. The kingdom of heaven points to the citizenship of heaven, and the kingdom of God points to the rulership, power, ability, strength, and authority that the citizens are to live under as relating to his kingdom.

Jesus displayed this truth throughout the three years we have recorded of his ministry. He represented the kingdom of heaven as being a citizen of it. Therefore, the power, authority, strength, and might of the kingdom of God were always on display in his life. It is to be the same way in our everyday life. As we take our places as citizens of heaven, we will see the power, rule, and authority of the kingdom displayed in, to, and through us.

No matter what country we live in, the natural citizenship of that particular country covers only the natural side of our being, with no provisions for us spiritually. The world was never created to give us our place, identity, or purpose. These are to come from our relationship with God as our spiritual Father. We are spirit beings (John 4:24, 6:63). We need to understand how important it is for us to embrace the reality of being citizens of the kingdom of heaven and living under its authority like Jesus did.

There is no law of the land or of any government that can overrule the spiritual laws established for us. Inside of our bodies is the real us, the spiritual us. It's from within that we live life as citizens of heaven. Genesis 1:26 says, "God said, Let us make man in our image and after our likeness, and let them have dominion...," God made man free; he created him with the right and authority to freely choose to obey God's commandments. Adam was to live freely and obey God, sharing in the intimacy of the relationship they had.

Adam was not a citizen because he was not born—he was created when God breathed into his nostrils the breath of life and he became a living soul. God placed in Adam the responsibility of representing the rule of God in the earth. Through Adam, the spiritual rule of heaven was his responsibility to establish in the lives of those of us who came after him. We were to be born just as free as he was.

Through the unseen kingdom that Adam represented, he was to rule over all the other kingdoms that God made. He started right. He did everything by the Word and presence of God. He possessed everything he needed to rule the natural kingdom from the unseen kingdom he was walking in. He began his life eating from the tree of life that represents the life of God and his rule over man. God treated him as if he was a citizen of the kingdom of heaven. Then we see him commit the act of treason.

Treason is the crime of a citizen of one country helping that country's enemies or trying to destroy the country's government. The *Online Etymological Dictionary* says it's "an act of betraying; a betrayal of trust; a breach of faith, a handing over, delivery, a surrender of. Treason is the violation by a subject of his allegiance to his sovereign or the state."[2] Man was created to have a loyal heart, a heart that is dependent upon and trusts God. In Genesis 2, Adam was given instructions about guarding and keeping the garden to protect God's interest in the earth, as well as keeping himself safe.

There were and are enemies to the plan and purpose of God. They are spiritual, not natural. The enemy is the same today as then—the devil and his demons (Isaiah 14; Ezekiel 28; and Revelation 12). In modern times, he still wants to keep us away from heaven's reality and rule over us.

When Adam died in the garden, he died spiritually to God and became a child of the devil. He was then born into slavery and lost his freedom to choose, as well as all rights to life. The last state of the first Adam is the state into which we were born. But God had a plan to redeem us (Genesis 3:15; Colossians 1:13). Jesus's death was not designed just to forgive our sins; by his blood, we became citizens of heaven.

We can't see or contact this kingdom with our natural senses; however, we can see the results of what is taking place spiritually by what is displayed naturally. The kingdom-against-kingdom power struggle is still going on in the world today. Adam's act of treason did not originate with the eating of the fruit but in the changing of his heart from believing the truth to believing a lie. He was commissioned to guard and keep his heart like he was to guard and keep the garden.

The moment he ate the fruit is when he acted on the change of heart. Instead of keeping and guarding, he was passive as his wife conversed with the devil through the serpent (Gen. 3:1–4). (If you did not know this, the devil was kicked out of heaven and his glory removed because he had attempted a rebellion in heaven.) Thus the devil turned his rage against all that God had restored and the man he had placed in charge. Adam was the first man to be born from life unto death. When he disobeyed, he died spiritually and became a slave of the kingdom of darkness. He lost all rights; he had no protection, no provision, no hope of immigrating or becoming a refugee, and no way on his own to get out of the state he was born into and back into the kingdom he was to represent.

Being born again changes all of this. We are to work the Word until the reality of our heavenly citizenship is rooted and grounded in our thinking by faith. Hebrews 11:13–16 says,

"These all died in faith, not having received the promises, but having seen them afar off, and were persuaded of them, and embraced them, and confessed that they were strangers and pilgrims on the earth. For they that say such things declare plainly that they seek a country. And truly, if they had been mindful of that country from whence they came out, they might have had opportunity to have returned. But now they desire a better country, that is, an heavenly: wherefore God is not ashamed to be called their God: for he hath prepared for them a city."

These were the Old Covenant believers. By faith they saw the reality of heaven, which we are now citizens of. Ask the question, Why would one establish a city? The only answer could be, For citizens. They saw our day and went looking for it. We are living in what they saw by faith.

Thus, living by faith is vitally important. The citizenship we have from God can be seen and accessed only by faith. When Adam committed the act of treason, his faith was perverted into fear, and he was born of fear and estranged from the rights to the citizenship of heaven. Ephesians 2:12 says, "That at that time ye were without Christ, being aliens from the commonwealth of Israel, and strangers from the covenants of promise, having no hope, and without God in the world."

The word *commonwealth* in this verse means "citizen" or "citizenship." *Vines Expository Dictionary* says it means "a member of a city or state or the inhabitant of a country or district."[3] *Holman Christian Standard Bible* (HCSB) says of Ephesians 2:12, "At that time you were without the Messiah, excluded from the citizenship of Israel, and foreigners to the covenants of the promise, without hope and without God in the world."

However, everyone who has called upon the name of Jesus was saved and instantly became a citizen of heaven. We are not only to believe we are Christians; along with this truth is the fact that we were made citizens of the kingdom of heaven. A man is either a citizen of heaven or not. There are no immigration statuses, refugees, or visas as in this physical world. Citizenship is attained only by the new birth.

Because of past experiences, we may think the earthly government we live under is for the rich, plays favoritism, or just plainly doesn't care about us because we don't meet its criteria in that we're not the "one percenters." Our enemy uses this ploy; he wants us to disrespect the government of the land in which we live, knowing that if he can convince us to have a negative attitude against it, we will have the same mind-set against the spiritual kingdom God set up for us.

Our mind-set should be the one God has instructed us to have concerning the natural government so that we will operate in agreement with the unseen rule of heaven over us. Notice the heart of the following scriptures.

> They say unto him, Caesar's. Then saith he unto them, Render therefore unto Caesar the things which are Caesar's; and unto God the things that are God's. (Matt. 22:21)

> Let every soul be subject unto the higher powers. For there is no power but of God: the powers that be are ordained of God. Whosoever, therefore, resisteth the power, resisteth the ordinance of God: and they that resist shall receive to themselves damnation. For rulers are not a terror to good works, but to the evil. Wilt thou then not be afraid of the power? do that which is good, and thou shalt have praise of the same: For he is the minister of God to thee for good. But if thou do that which is evil, be afraid; for he beareth not the sword in vain: for he is the minister of God, a revenger to execute wrath upon him that doeth evil. Wherefore ye must need be subject, not only for wrath but also for conscience sake. For this cause pay ye tribute also: for they are God's ministers, attending continually upon this very thing. Render therefore to all their dues: tribute to whom tribute is due; custom to whom custom; fear to whom fear; honour to whom honour, but in the Kingdom God has for us, we are all one, we are equally the same in his eyes, the blood of Jesus was shed for all, giving us all equal rights to the blessings of God. (Romans 13:1–7)

> I exhort, therefore, that, first of all, supplications, prayers, intercessions, and giving of thanks, be made for all men; For kings, and for all that are in authority; that we may lead a quiet and peaceable life in all godliness and honesty. For this is good and acceptable in the sight of God our Saviour. (1 Tim. 2:1–3)

These instructions are for the natural governments we are under in our countries, but remember—we have a spiritual government that we are to respect more highly.

> For unto us a child is born, unto us a son is given: and the government shall be upon his shoulder: and his name shall be called Wonderful, Counsellor, The mighty God, The everlasting Father, The Prince of Peace. Of the increase of his government and peace there shall be no end, upon the throne of David, and upon his kingdom, to order it, and to establish it with judgment and with justice from henceforth even forever. The zeal of the LORD of hosts will perform this. (Isa. 9:6–7)

We naturally are citizens of the countries we were born in, but spiritually we who have received Jesus as our personal Savior and Lord are citizens of heaven. It's not about what we have done; it's about what God has established for all who will believe him. And he calls those who believe citizens of heaven.

All things natural have their origins in the spirit. Even though natural laws may be against us, these laws cannot trump, override, or neutralize the spiritual laws of our being citizens of heaven. All humanity is seeking to find the perfect place to live, fit in, be a part of, and live a prosperous life. No natural government can do this for us; we can find this life only in the kingdom of heaven.

He promised to provide our every need and to protect, defend, sustain, keep, lead, guide, help, heal, and prosper us in every way.

He promised that we would have his love, mercy, favor, forgiveness, grace, might, power, and anointing upon our life. Child of God, it does not matter what the natural world gives us or how it looks down upon us, labels us, or snubs us. The kingdom of heaven will never and can never handle its citizens this way.

Jesus was a citizen of Bethlehem naturally. Matthew 2:1, declares, "Now when Jesus was born in Bethlehem of Judaea in the days of Herod the king..."

Yet, in the earth, Jesus's highest priority was living like a citizen of heaven. Paul, who was called Saul before his conversion, used his natural citizenship to get to Rome to see Caesar because God's will for him was to represent the interests of the kingdom of heaven there.

Ephesians 2:19 says, "Now therefore ye are no more strangers and foreigners, but fellow-citizens with the saints, and of the household of God." This means that we are not strangers or foreigners to the kingdom of heaven; we are citizens. We are not on the outside of his will any longer. He made us of his kingdom. God says that we are fellow citizens with the saints. We are of his household.

Remember the various ways to become a citizen. The two that apply to us are being born in the country and being born to a parent who is a natural citizen of the country. God has done both. All who have called upon the name of Jesus are born from above (John 3), and he has grafted us into being Jews spiritually so that we can receive their blessings (Romans 3, 11). God is our spiritual Father.

Under the Old Covenant, the Jewish nation could never be citizens of heaven because Jesus had to give his life for them to be born again. However, under the New Covenant, they had the power of the kingdom displayed upon their life. If you have been born again, then you are a citizen of heaven, holding all the rights and privileges of the Lord Jesus Christ himself. Our constitution is the Word of God; here is where we find our rights and privileges as citizens of heaven's reality.

In this world, we are to make our stand as citizens of heaven. We are to live in its rights and privileges and enjoy the abundant life Jesus said we are to have—spirit, soul, and body. Being a citizen of heaven is an honor that God wants us to embrace with all our heart, for he chose it for us.

Here is a pledge of allegiance for citizens of heaven.

> I pledge allegiance to the Anointed Christ,
> the representative of the government of heaven.
> I pledge my loyalty to his sovereign rule,
> declaring him to be my Lord.
> By faith I live as a united nation under God,
> being inseparable from him,
> living in the liberty and righteousness of the covenant
> blood of Jesus for all.

Chapter 8

God's View of His Word Our Constitution

In the United States and most other countries, there are laws that cover every citizen. Men established the laws of the United States for the operation of this wonderful country. Sadly, the majority of citizens are in the dark about these laws because they do not have a working knowledge of their constitutional rights and privileges, other than the freedom of speech, the right to bear arms, and the freedom of religion. I am talking about the Constitution of the United States; this is the backbone of uniformity, responsibility, rights, and privileges for the government and the citizens of America.

The laws of the land are based on or subject to it. Our constitution is the law of all laws in America. It defines the government of America and how this entity is to function at the federal and state levels. It details its purposes and boundaries. The constitution consists of the preamble, seven articles, and twenty-seven amendments—of which we, the citizens of America, should have a working knowledge.

These laws cover us only on the physical level, but there is another constitution that covers us spirit, soul, and body. This constitution is established on the nature of God. It covers the entire operation of the kingdom of heaven and its citizens. Isaiah 9:6–7 declares, "For unto us a child is born, unto us a son is given: and the government shall be upon his shoulder: and his name shall be called Wonderful, Counsellor, The mighty God, The everlasting Father, The Prince of Peace. Of the increase of his government and peace there shall be no end, upon the throne of David, and upon his kingdom, to order it, and to establish it with judgment and with justice from henceforth even forever. The zeal of the LORD of hosts will perform this." This verse is referring to Jesus.

Notice the phrase, "And the government shall be upon his shoulder." Jesus lived in complete agreement with the principles of the kingdom of heaven while on the earth; he bore the responsibility of keeping every commandment contained in it. He had a working understanding of what was legal and what was not. He succeeded where the first Adam came up short.

Now, regarding this verse, we have been trained to think about it only during the Christmas holidays and have not taken it as a present reality that impacts our life for the greater good of the kingdom of heaven. The first Adam was entrusted with it and committed high treason against it, allowing the devil to have dominion over him and us.

After Adam sinned, God promised a redeemer (Genesis 3:15), who was Christ Jesus and who bore this government upon his shoulder. When he was born into the earth realm, he demonstrated the governmental rule of heaven in, upon, and through a man. He displayed the ins and outs of how to live in this kingdom reality. He walked in love, he lived by faith, he saw himself righteously, and he depended on God's grace. He believed he was the anointed one. He lived as one who possesses the presence of God, his life and nature, and the ability to use the authority of the kingdom of God.

As citizens of heaven, God gave us our constitution—it's his Word. It's the ultimate law, the law that governs every other law, be it spiritual or natural. The word *constitution* means "a body of fundamental principles or established precedents according to which a state or other organization is acknowledged to be governed."[1] It refers to the system of beliefs and laws by which a country, state, or organization is governed or a document that describes this system; it means an established law, custom, or ordinance. The Word of God is to be seen as more than just a book. It's our constitution, by which we can understand the operation of the kingdom of heaven and all the rights enjoined unto us. The difference between God's law and the law of the land is that God's is perfect. What fits one fits all, and what he will do for one he will do for all who choose to believe.

Jesus showed us how to walk in our God-given constitutional rights for three years of his recorded life. He was raised from the dead to preside over its implementation in and upon our life. As citizens, when we understand what is rightfully ours by the Word of God, we will live life as God created us to live.

As children of God and citizens of heaven, it is to our advantage to learn the legal rights, the principles that God established for us to live by. We must bring our thinking up to his truth by renewing our mind to what he says is to be for us. Remember, Jesus said, "Render unto Caesar that which is Caesar's and unto God that which is God's" (Mark 12:17). These two individuals represented their respective governments in the world. Jesus did not deny the government of Caesar; he told us that they are not one and the same and that we should respect both.

Government in the Hebrew language means "empire."[2] According to the *Online Etymology Dictionary*, this word means "rule, authority, kingdom, imperial rule, a command, authority, control, power, supreme power, sole dominion, military authority, and/or realm."[3]

What we are being led to see is a glimpse of God's governing rule over his children. His rule is supreme; it's right. His rule keeps, sustains, and affords divine protection, provision, health, and peace in every area of our life. And most of all, it affords intimacy with him. We may never have an audience with our president, but we are guaranteed an audience with God.

The laws of God are not about do's and don'ts, as I learned from my religious upbringing. His laws are intended for our total well-being. They are designed for us to come to understand how to order our steps in agreement with his will so we can experience his life now. Since you are reading this book, now is the time for you to look up and believe. You have every right to live in heaven's reality for you.

Use the Word to change your view of yourself. You are the King's child. You are royalty to him; you are his heir and a joint heir with Christ. Laws are the arms of a constitution. So when the Bible speaks about the laws of God, let's translate this into the word *constitution*. Joshua 1:8 says, "This book of the law shall not depart out of thy mouth; but thou shalt meditate therein day and night, that thou mayest observe to do according to all that is written therein: for then thou shalt make thy way prosperous, and then thou shalt have good success."

This verse does not sound like a law of do's and don'ts. If we do what this verse says, we will not do those things that God says are against his will for us, and the things we used to do will be memories of our past. Now for the translation: This book of the constitution, the Bible, the Word of God, the constitution of heaven that represents God's rule over us and what we are to expect from him as we live in submission unto him, is to be in our mouth.

The Word of God is our divine constitution; it is our good news of all God has enjoined unto us. The problem I had for years was that I carried the same mind-set and attitude concerning natural laws, which was truly about the constitution from which all laws came, and carried them over into the laws of God because of the view I had of myself. I did not see what the Word was to represent to me until many years later, but when the light came on, things began to change inside of me, in my heart. Changes are still taking place, and my walk is so different than when I started.

If you can identify with this, I am here to tell you that you have hope. Your day of liberation is upon you. You are about to enter into the reality of seeing your enemies no more and experiencing life the way you were created by God to live—under his rule.

When we have something stolen and the thief gets arrested, the police ask us if we want to press charges. Doing so is using our constitutional rights. We are to do the same to the devil, the thief; we are to exercise our God-given constitutional rights against him and not be afraid of being retaliated against. He has no power to resist the authority leveled against him.

In Luke 10:19, Jesus said, "Behold, I give unto you power to tread on serpents and scorpions, and over all the power of the enemy: and nothing shall by any means hurt you." The first *power* means "authority," while the second *power* means "ability." The authority that Jesus is talking about here is the authority of the kingdom of God because we are citizens of the kingdom of heaven.

Thus, when we take a stand on our godly constitutional rights, the devil has no answer for the one who backs up his Word in our life. Ask yourself, What has God ever created that is not subject to the authority of his Word? The answer is "Nothing." All things are subject unto him, and he has given us his Word to declare by faith and get the same results as he does.

We all were led to believe that our ability was enough, but it's not. This is the work of the devil, intended to keep us blinded from the truth that we possess the rights and privileges to speak the Word he must obey. We are to live by our position of being in Jesus; this makes us children and citizens, which means we walk in his authority, the Spirit of God. We are more than what we see, and we have a constitution based on the will of God.

Notice what Jesus said in Luke 11:20: "But if I with the finger of God cast out devils, no doubt the kingdom of God is come upon you." Jesus likened the finger of God to the kingdom of God, the authority of heaven. Jesus walked in this authority of heaven, and all devils were in subjection to the word of the constitution he spoke. Matthew records it this way in Chapter 12, verse 28: "But if I cast out devils by the Spirit of God, then the kingdom of God is come unto you." Here Jesus tells us that the Spirit of God is the manifested authority of the kingdom of God. The Spirit of God backs up and makes good the constitutional rights of its citizens who live by faith; thus, through faith we declare our God-given rights like Jesus did.

What did Jesus speak? He spoke the supreme law, the mother of all laws. He spoke what people had the legal right to be or have in life. We must believe that we have the same constitutional rights with

God, and the Spirit of God will do the same in our life as we read that he did in the life of Jesus. The deception that our ability is enough will only cause us to live life frustrated, feeling trapped, discouraged, and on edge because nothing works like we think it should.

However, getting the truth in our heart as children of God and citizens of heaven, we can now focus on the rights and privileges given us by him. He positioned us to live as citizens of heaven. We are to take his word, trusting in the authority of the kingdom of God to restore all we thought we lost, redeem all things stolen, and make our life as the Bible says, days of heaven on earth. In reading Deuteronomy 11:18–25, notice verse 21, which states, "That your days may be multiplied, and the days of your children, in the land which the LORD sware unto your fathers to give them, as the days of heaven upon the earth."

I believe the writer is referring to the Garden of Eden before man fell. The garden represented the spiritual reality that man was created to live in. God has not changed his mind for us under the New Testament. We live in the better of the two covenants. We live in the reality of what those under the Old Covenant could only do in part, but the Law, the Word, our constitution is here in full force to operate in our life.

We have these rights not because of anything we have done but because we are born-again children of God. He expects us to take his Word, get it in our heart, and let it become our knowledge, wisdom, and understanding of our constitutional, legal rights given us by God.

Like in the natural, so in the spirit—if we do not have a working knowledge of the rights God has provided for us, others can take advantage of us by imposing their will, their selfishness, and their lawlessness upon us. As citizens of heaven with divine rights, we do not have to passively stand by and allow the devil to run over us. We don't have to continue to put up with his lies, deceptions, and trickery. We have the legal jurisdiction over all he can do. We are the ones backed by the government of heaven.

Take him to court, and declare your legal rights before God. He encourages us to put him in remembrance. Let us plead together—we are to declare that we may be justified. In every situation we face, we are to go to God, reminding him of the rights he established for us as his children, and we are to plead or judge together what we face based on those rights. Then we declare those rights as the answer, and he says we may be justified based on our rights being violated.

It's not like God does not remember that this is one of his ways of getting us into faith. He responds to faith; he responds to our believing and trusting in what he declared to be for us, and he will make our enemy restore unto us not only what was stolen but seven times more. This makes faith vitally important. By faith we walk in our constitutional rights of heaven. All born-again believers, whether they were born again one day or many years ago, all have the same constitutional, legal, God-given rights to live in heaven's reality on earth.

The Word of God is key. It's the book of our constitution, of our rights and privileges. Consider Joshua 1:8 again: "This book of the law shall not depart out of thy mouth; but thou shalt meditate therein day and night, that thou mayest observe to do according to all that is written therein: for then thou shalt make thy way prosperous, and then thou shalt have good success."

This book of the law contains the constitutional rights of citizens of heaven, and we are to keep these rights in our mouth, speaking them out because it's the way God sees us. So we don't wait until a problem or pressure comes upon us; we speak our God-given rights out by faith. Faith is not a get-out-of-jail-free card. It is a remover of all things used against us to keep us from living life on God's terms.

Then we are told to meditate on our constitutional rights day and night, observing to do all that is written therein concerning us, for then we will make our way prosperous. The light will be turned on in our heart, and we will see how we are seen by God. At the end of this journey, we will have good success—or, as the *Amplified Bible* (AMP) says, in part, in Joshua 1:8, "... and then you shall deal wisely and have good success."

The Word is the key to our success and to dealing wisely in the affairs of life. We must measure ourselves by our citizenship in heaven. Romans 12:2 says, "And be not conformed to this world: but be ye transformed by the renewing of your mind, that ye may prove what is that good, and acceptable, and perfect, will of God."

The battle is in the mind, not in our behavior. When we allow our minds to be transformed, our behavior will then change. The standard of this world's system is not the standard by which we are to judge ourselves anymore. God provided us a new standard to live up to—Jesus. We are in him, meaning that all he is, so are we—spirit, soul, and body. Through Jesus, we have the legal right to see and live as God declared for us.

Our enemy is afraid of us standing in our covenant rights. He wants to hinder us from knowing anything that is legally ours. He works to keep us ignorant about the rights we have to live free from his control. God set us free from the power of darkness and has translated us into the kingdom of his dear Son. Isn't that wonderful news? It does not matter where we came from. Where we were once spiritual slaves, now we are spiritually free. Where we were once paupers, now are we royalty. Where we were once cursed, now we are blessed.

At one point, we were not known by God, but now in Christ Jesus, we are his sons and daughters. We are his heirs and are joint heirs with Christ. We are citizens of heaven, and the Word is our constitution.

In Psalm 1:1–3, we read,

> Blessed is the man that walketh not in the counsel of the ungodly, nor standeth in the way of sinners, nor sitteth in the seat of the scornful. But his delight is in the law of the LORD; and in his law doth he meditate day and night. And he shall be like a tree planted by the rivers of water, that bringeth forth his fruit in his season; his leaf also shall not wither; and whatsoever he doeth shall prosper.

Verse 1 tells us that God has a blessing for us if we do not remain conformed to the ways of the world, which we have come to depend upon. From there he tells us where to place our delight—in his law, his constitution, in which we are to meditate day and night. The result is becoming planted, bearing fruit, and being prosperous in all we do. It's very important for us to grasp the rights and privileges given unto us. Our constitution is the will of God for our life. This constitution sets the boundaries for our life, and in them we are to abide.

Jesus lived in this reality. He was fixed, fruitful, and always covered, and so should we be. Hebrews 8:10 declares to us, "For this is the covenant that I will make with the house of Israel after those days, saith the Lord; I will put my laws into their mind, and write them in their hearts and I will be to them a God, and they shall be to me a people."

God's desire is for his laws to be in our mind and written in our heart. As we give voice to what he tells us and meditate on it, we allow him to put his laws in our mind and write them on our heart. Laws are what govern our life in the state or country in which we live, and it is the same with the kingdom of God.

The laws of the kingdom of heaven are the manifestation of the constitution we have been placed into. He's given us his laws to govern our life; he wants us to think, speak, and act like him in all situations with the confidence to believe him like Jesus did. Jesus knew that all of heaven supported him, and he is our example of what God is looking to do in our life as well.

We have a judicial judge, who is our Father; Jesus is our executive officer; and the Holy Spirit is our mediator. All three are on our side. They long to enforce the constitutional rights they determined us to have. We are not alone; we have unseen help for every issue we face in life. These laws tell us what is legal to be in our life and what is not—health for sickness, acceptance for rejection, life for death, joy for sadness, strength for weakness, prosperity for lack, hope for despair. The list is unending.

The only thing we must learn to do is speak our constitutional rights and follow the instructions given to us. We are to look at what Jesus did more than what we have done. God is for us, so who can be against us? He is listening to hear his Word come out of our mouths and looking to see it firmly fixed and established in our mind and heart.

Believe we are citizens of heaven, believe we have God-given rights to possess in life now, believe all of heaven is behind us, believe we have the right to live as God declared, and believe in our constitution of heaven, the Word of God. Let's strive to view the Word as our constitution and see it as the mother of all laws—laws God has given us to govern every aspect of our life. We have the legal right to have all the word (our constitution) says established in our life, not later but right now while we are on this earth.

View the Word of God as our legal constitution. We can and should stand up in faith and boldly declare all it contains about us. If God took the time to say it, we can take the time to speak it by faith. We are what the Word says we are, we can do what the Word says we can do, and we have what the Word says we have.

The government of the kingdom of heaven is like no other government that ever existed. God's kingdom is run by love—this means that every commandment, law, principle, word, and instruction comes from love. As children, we live under the constitution of pure love, which shows no partiality. This love is extended to every citizen, and he has shed it abroad in our heart by the Holy Ghost. It is the love who promised to send Jesus our Redeemer, the love who promised the Holy Spirit, and the love that cannot fail. This love only knows equality.

In this world's system, it appears laws are divvied out to its citizens based on position, gender, skin color, money, education, and so on, but it is not so in the kingdom of God. We are all one, and he applies the authority of his kingdom to all who believe, without respect of persons. Jesus showed us how a citizen is to live; he understood his rights and never bowed down to any law that opposed the will of God for his life.

We have no account of Jesus's being poor, sick, depressed, fearful, in bondage, or the like. He set the standard by imposing his will in the will of God. Death could not resist him and the grave could not hold him. Children of God, believe it is illegal for sickness to be in your body, believe it is illegal for poverty to run your life, and believe it is illegal for anything the devil imposes upon you to exercise dominion over you. View yourself as a citizen of heaven, take the time to learn your constitutional rights, and walk in your God-given freedom and victory.

Chapter 9

Our New View

The view or image we have of ourselves is of utmost importance to how we live, what we can do, and how we will function here on this earth. God did not save us so we would continue struggling on earth as if we were still bound to sin. The issue we face is not about our natural side; rather it is about our spiritual side as it pertains to the view, perception, or image we have of ourselves. Inside each and every one of us is an image of how we see ourselves.

The issues of our life begin in our heart. Proverbs 4:23 says, "Keep your heart with all diligence, for out of it are the issues of life." We have spent most of our life trying to outlive the images we have in our heart only to find ourselves stuck in its gravitational pull, keeping us bound to the dynamics of its control over our heart and mind.

We spend much time with our focus primarily on our body, while on the inside is sadness, depression, ill feelings, and the like, being too embarrassed to say anything about it. Some contemplate suicide, others turn to drugs or alcohol, and some go to the extreme of doing harm to themselves and ultimately completing suicide.

Religion has kept us from seeing ourselves as we are seen by God and left us thinking there is nothing we can do here to change anything about our present life. However, God's will is for us to see ourselves in our heart as he sees us in Christ. This is to be the core of our heart. Say this: "I am determined to see myself as God sees me and live like it is so."

Joshua 1:7 says, "Only be thou strong and very courageous, that thou mayest observe to do according to all the law, which Moses my servant commanded thee: turn not from it to the right hand or to the left, that thou mayest prosper whithersoever thou goest."

God did not tell Joshua he was strong; he told him to *be* strong and very courageous. When he believed about himself what God said to him, God assisted him in doing everything he said for him to do. We must act like we are strong and very courageous even when it appears we are facing utter defeat, and he will assist us.

As Joshua developed the inner image of how God saw him in his heart, we must do the same. We are to believe that we have on the inside of ourselves everything God gave us to have so we can allow him to fulfill his will in our life.

He will assist us as we live by faith, like with Moses, Joshua, David, Jesus, Peter, Paul, and so forth. He is waiting for us to take him at his word as we arise and see ourselves in our heart as he says we are. He has a new view of us, and he calls us all to depend on it. We must develop the image of ourselves in our heart and mind as our Father God says we are.

The only person who did not have a problem with the view, image, or perception of himself was Jesus. He knew who he was, and so did the devil. In Matthew 4:3, the devil attacked Jesus first about the image he had about himself. Jesus's body was hungry, but being subtle, the devil attacked him spiritually, starting with, "If you be the Son of God." Jesus knew who he was, but the devil first and foremost attacked Jesus's image of himself. Why? He wanted to see if the truth was rooted and grounded in his heart.

Our response should be the same as Jesus's response. We are to say what God has written for us. Notice that Jesus said only what was written; he did not come up with some fancy words, and he said, "It is written." Jesus responded like a son who trusted in what his Father said. What we say must be what God said for us to say.

When we speak by faith, we are speaking from the view God

has of us. Life will be a struggle if we don't see ourselves correctly. By faith, we are to believe we are what God says we are. Speaking what the Word says will eventually take hold in our heart because faith comes by hearing and hearing by the Word of God.

The value of our life can be measured only by what God used to save us—the blood of Jesus. We are not worthless; we do have a purpose for being here on earth. Regardless of what others have said or do say about us, remember this: we did not come from them. We are a spirit, we came from God, and we are what he says we are.

John 3:16 states, "For God so loved the world, that he gave his only begotten Son, that whosoever believes in him should not perish but have everlasting life." Brothers and sisters, the moment we were born again, we were born of God's life and nature. Begin to say right now, "Spiritually, I have the life and nature of God; I have eternal life." Say it because faith comes by hearing and hearing by the Word of God. Say it, and your feelings and emotions will eventually catch up to this truth.

One may ask the question, "What does eternal, everlasting life—the life and nature of God—look like?" This is a good question, and the answer is that we have four books in the Bible about the life of Jesus. He is the expression of eternal, everlasting life. The way Jesus lived was the manifestation of the life and nature of God that was in him (Hebrews 1:3).

Our new view according to God is that we are his children. In 2 Corinthians 5:17, we read, "Therefore if any man be in Christ, he is a new creature: old things are passed away; behold, all things are become new." Spiritually speaking, everything about us has become new. Mentally and physically, nothing changed, but the part of us that is spiritual is brand new. We must believe that we are a spirit, and through the new spiritual birth, we now possess the life and nature of God—not in the sweet by-and-by, but right now. Romans 8:16–17 tells us, "The Spirit itself beareth witness with our spirit, that we are the children of God: And if children, then heirs; heirs of God, and joint-heirs with Christ; if so be that we suffer with him, that we may also be glorified together."

Verse 16 informs us of the new birth; the Spirit bears witness with our spirit. The moment we received Jesus as our personal Savior and Lord, we became children of God. We became new creatures in Christ Jesus. We are not what we used to be; now we are spiritually alive, having the life and nature of God. In verse 17, we are told the position we have with our Father God. He declares that we are his children, which makes us heirs, and not just any heir, but an heir of God and a joint-heir with Christ.

What God has done for us through the Lord Jesus Christ is what our new view is established upon. We are not to continue to view ourselves from the natural position anymore or as the world programmed us to believe. The world system knows nothing about God and what he has made us to be in Christ. Ask yourself, If God created man in his image and after his likeness, isn't that the way he would always see them? And if the answer is yes, then if anything caused man to destroy the image and likeness God made him to be, wouldn't God do everything needed to restore the correct view back to him?

The answer would be yes, yes, yes. He did this through the new birth process. Our new view is of Christ Jesus, and this new view is of us being the sons and daughters of Almighty God. He has done everything needed for us to have the correct view of ourselves restored. Now he expects us to believe we are what he says we are and we have what he says we have, not because of anything we have done; it's all based on who he is and what he has done for us.

Man is a tripartite being. The real us possess the life and nature of God; upon being born again, we possess the same spiritual DNA as God. The first Adam lost the right to this truth, but the last Adam came to restore unto us the right to the new view. The issue is not what we go through, what we have done to ourselves, or what others did to us. Rather, it's what image we live by, the view we have of ourselves to address the issues in our life.

The view we have of ourselves is what determines whether we have success over or continue to succumb to the issues of life. Jesus, in telling us what the great commandments are, said that the second one is like unto the first. He said that we are to love our neighbors as ourselves. The degree to which we love ourselves is the degree to which we should love our neighbors.

In developing the new view of ourselves, we must learn to love ourselves. I recall the time when I asked the Lord to help me understand this verse because I saw how others used it to show how to love their neighbors, and it did not sit well in my heart. They used this verse when there was jealousy, bitterness, strife, or resentment at work but never to demonstrate a way of life. What people were encouraged to do was cook something, take the neighbor out to eat, or even buy something. You can see how this could get expensive.

People's attitudes remained the same. There was no genuine love displayed because this behavior is not what God instructs us to do, and I did not want to do what was not pleasing to him. The Lord is not reactive; he is proactive. He wants us to be proactive concerning our heart, and buying food—or buying anything—is not it! He is about restoring our heart to its destined state.

What he told me was for me to separate my *who* from my *do*. He said I am not what I do; what I do is the result of how I see myself, who I think I am, or the view I have of myself. He said that if I viewed myself rightly, then I would do right. It's not the doing that would change me; rather, when I see myself the way he says I am, change will take place in what I do.

Love our neighbors as we love ourselves. Before we can love our neighbors, we must first learn to love ourselves. Instead of looking for someone to love us, we're it; no one can love us for us. We are to learn to love ourselves from the inside first. This requires us to submit our heart to the new view God purchased for us. By establishing his view of us, we can fulfill the law of love he commands us to walk in. The view he has given unto us is an image of his love, so we can love others as he does by representing his will here in the earth.

Can we love our neighbors as God requires us to? Yes, we can. To love our neighbors, we must first love ourselves. This truth is not something we have majored in yet. How can we love others if we don't love ourselves? Jesus always walked in love. Even on the cross, he prayed for the forgiveness of those who crucified him. What an act of love.

God has a view of us in his heart that he longs to develop in our heart. His view of us is us being just like him. Jesus said to Philip, "If you have seen me, you have seen the Father" (John 14:9). When this view is rooted and grounded in our heart, we will shine as bright lights in this dark world. I believe we need to focus on the image that God created us to live by. We need to make sure this image is compatible with our spirit so we can represent him like Jesus did.

He knows which people, out of all those born into the earth, will accept his offer to become his sons and daughters. He knows when everyone will receive Jesus as his or her personal Savior and Lord. He is omniscient, or all knowing. He does not determine whom he will save, but he does know who all will call out to be saved. He also predestined or predetermined that all who would receive Jesus would be conformed into the image of Jesus.

God's will for us is to look spiritually just like Jesus, and we do. We are born spiritually alive unto God, and now the image of Jesus is to be formed, shaped, or established in our heart. With his new view established in our heart, our spirit will then have access to it and we will accomplish his will for our life.

Our battles are in our mind, not our brain. Our brain is for our body, but our mind is for our spirit. Our brains know nothing about the new image God has for us because they cannot operate above the natural. Our mind is spiritual, and it can be reshaped and conformed to possess the image of Christ. We read in 2 Corinthians 10:5, "Casting down imaginations, and every high thing that exalteth itself against the knowledge of God, and bringing into captivity every thought to the obedience of Christ."

Imaginations, every high thing and every thought are all spiritual, and we have to address them at the same level on which they exist. Faith is the tool we have been given to reach them as we stand on his Word. We must trust that the Word is the source we are to believe. All imaginations, every high thing and every thought we are in bondage to, we possess the power of God to set us free. These strongholds are directly connected to the inner view by which we see ourselves. The first stronghold we are told to cast down is imaginations. *Imagination*[1] comes from the word *image,* or we can say how we view ourselves. Thus, how we see ourselves in our heart is the life we will live.

As we resist the perverted image of the first Adam and establish the new image of the last Adam, we will develop new imaginations to live by. Instead of living by every high thing, we will become humble and submissive, and our thoughts will agree with the will of God. This is why he tells us in Ephesians 4:22–24, "That ye put off concerning the former conversation the old man, which is corrupt according to the deceitful lusts; and be renewed in the spirit of your mind; and that ye put on the new man, which after God is created in righteousness and true holiness."

Child of God, being saved includes a new view for you. God's plan is for all of us who are his children to shine like Jesus did in the world. We are called to walk in love one toward another so we can experience life as he says it is to be, help those inside the family to grow to another degree of glory in Christ, and help those outside the family to come into it.

The lies are that we cannot change, we can't do anything about anything, we're just victims, and we should keep a stiff upper lip and just accept it. At the other extreme are those who put it all off on God because no one knows what he will do. Ask yourself this question: Why would God save us but let our life remain the same? Would he not want every aspect of our life saved? The answer would be yes.

God is looking to save our heart now in this dispensation of grace. We must believe that he can do in our life as he promised. James 1:21 declares, "Wherefore lay apart all filthiness and superfluity of naughtiness, and receive with meekness the engrafted word, which is able to save your souls." In Ephesians 4:23, we read, "And be renewed in the in the spirit of your mind;" God wants both of them changed. When does he want our soul saved and mind renewed? Now.

The Word is the foundation of the change he is looking to accomplish. As we read, study, meditate, confess, pray, and act like the Word is true, he will be given what he needs to bring about in our heart the changes he has his heart set on doing. And in allowing him to change our heart, the new view he has for us is established.

Proverbs 4:23 instructs us, "Keep thy heart with all diligence; for out of it are the issues of life." What we have in life is directly linked to our heart. If what God says does not exist in our heart, it's impossible for us to have it in our life. Thus, we must get the Word in our heart. We are to keep, guard, protect, and maintain it with all diligence, for out of it comes the issues of our life.

If we do what the Word tells us, our heart will be filled with his truth, and from our heart we will have a new outcome in life. However, if we don't obey and keep his word, we will continue to experience what we have always known and continue to believe that the problem resides outside of us, blaming this or that and portraying ourselves as victims or at the mercy of something or someone else.

God made us his offspring, and he wants us to live like we are his children. He knows that when we allow him to establish his view of Jesus in our heart, we will see life through his eyes, fellowship intimately with him, and be open and willing to do what he wants when, where, and to whom he wants us to be his expression of love.

Brothers and sisters, image is everything to us and the life we live. God has a new view for us. It's a heavenly view from the heart of God to us, and as we work with him, this new view will take hold in our heart and propel us into a life we only dreamed could be for us.

So when you face another issue in your life, settle yourself, look internally first, and then ask the Lord to open the eyes of your understanding so you can see the view and image from which this issue is operating. Trust him, believe what you hear, and ask him to give you a witness (at least two or three) in his Word. And by his word, ask him to show you the view and image he has for you to develop in your heart, again going to his Word. When you get this information, write it down, cast down the one to be changed, and bring into captivity the thoughts connected to it. Believe you have the right view or image of yourself established in your heart, meditate on the Word that his new view of you is based on, and be patient. Change is coming, and you will soon have a new outlook on your life, knowing that you are viewing yourself as God sees you.

Chapter 10

Faith's View

The new view that God ordained for us to live by requires us to live by faith to bring it into reality from our spirit to our heart. Only when his view of us is in our heart will our everyday life begin to change for the better. All of the children of God are required by him to live the faith life. Romans 1:17 says in part, "..., The just shall live by faith." Hebrews 11:6 says in part "But without faith it is impossible to please him: ...." Romans 12:3 says in part, "..., according as God has dealt to every man the measure of faith." God has given to every man the measure of faith. We have all the faith we need, as born again children of God. He cannot give us any more faith than what he has already given.

We all have heard lessons and sermons, read books, and seen TV programs or DVDs on the subject. It is vitally important for us to understand how faith works. Here I want to share with you information on how to use faith. I knew the scriptures about faith, but it did not work for me like I thought it should. And when I cried out for revelation on this subject, God blessed me.

In Hebrews 11:1, he tells us, "Now faith is the substance of things hoped for, the evidence of things not seen." I say faith is the substance of things *I* hope for, completely changing it from how he had it written. I *Hope* is present tense, but *hoped* is past tense. Past tense means it's finished, accomplished, provided for by God. Faith is for those things God has already furnished. In 2 Corinthians 1:20, we read, "For all the promises of God in him are yea and in him Amen, unto the glory of God by us." Then, 2 Peter 1:3 says, "According as his divine power has given unto us all things that pertain unto life and godliness, through the knowledge of him that has called us to glory and virtue."

The word *past* is to indicate that we are to see ourselves presently possessing what God has provided for us. Faith is what we use to transfer the promises from our spirit and into our heart. How? By meditating, reading, using our imagination, and viewing ourselves with it. Faith's view is for us to develop an inner image or view of ourselves possessing the spiritual thing in our heart.

When we see it in our heart is when we will see it manifested in our life. Faith is the substance of spiritual things God promised us in Christ. It is one of the spiritual forces we are to develop in our heart to allow the image of the things to be brought into manifestation in our here and now.

First, we must believe God has put in our spirit all the things he promised us. Second, we must believe that faith is the means we have for the spiritual realities on the inside. And third, through faith, we develop these truths in our heart, from where our issues of life proceed. Only through faith can we bring our spirit and heart back into perfect alignment with the will of God.

We can believe we are everything God said we are in Christ. He made us to look just like Jesus spiritually, not when we get to heaven but right now. Wherever you live, in spite of all that's going on in your life, remember that we are to separate our *who* from our *do*. God knows who we are to him; he made us what he wanted us to be. Now the question is whether we see ourselves as he sees us. If we are born again, we are spiritually the children of God, and we need to get that image from our spirit and into our heart.

His Word is our key to obtaining the correct view of ourselves. Say this please: "How God sees me is in his Word." Hebrews 11:1 says, "Now faith is the substance of things hoped for; the evidence of the things not seen." The Word is our substance of the things God has given us, and the Word is our evidence of those things our senses cannot detect. Through faith we can see ourselves as God sees us and live in the reality of being his sons and daughters right here and now.

We have to make the transition from seeing ourselves as flesh to seeing ourselves as a spirit who are born of God, possessing his life and nature. God's will is for us to make his view of ourselves to be exactly like his. The images in our heart can be of faith or fear. Faith is not about the denomination we belong to; faith is for God. Every image in our heart is of spiritual origin.

The perverted image is of fear, and the godly image is of faith. God's will of and for us he connected to the faith he's given us. We don't have to work to obtain this truth; we are to submit humbly or yield our will to his, trusting that he can make our life as he says it is to be. He keeps every promise; he watches over every word to perform it. His Word will never fail, and it is the food for our spirit.

Remember, Romans 8:29 tells us, "For who he did foreknow he did predestinate, to be conformed to the image of his dear Son." God's view of us is the same view he has of Jesus. God is saying that, spiritually, we are exactly the same as Jesus to him. Faith allows us to look at what God provided, and the Spirit of God, through our faith, is working in our heart to conform the image of our heart to the image of Jesus so our spirit and heart can be one again.

Now we can see how important faith is. However, we have to come to see how to apply faith to our life or how to live by faith so we can walk in all the realities we have been given by the blood of Jesus. Our freedom is a thought away, and the promises of God are ours for the taking, I believed this when I started learning how to live by faith; you too will learn it and come to live by faith better than what you know.

If anyone knows how to live by faith, Jesus does, and here he is teaching us this truth. In Mark 11:22, Jesus said for us to have faith in God. Faith is not for natural things; faith is for God and the spiritual things he has put in our spirit for us to have in life. Through faith, we are making a spiritual exchange of what we presently have and believe in our heart, for what he has given us to be governed by.

In Mark 11:23, he says "Whosoever saith unto this mountain, be though removed and be though cast into the sea and shall not doubt in his heart, but shall believe, he shall have whatsoever he saith." We must say or repeat what God said. Child of God, you have the right to say what God said about you. Notice what he said was decreed before we ever showed up, and we are to say what he's said in the face of what we presently have. Faith's view only sees what God said.

Faith is the spiritual exchange between God and us; this exchange does not take place from the outside in, it takes place on the inside and then comes out. He led me to see the ingredients of faith more so than the operation of faith, for he knew that if I understood the ingredients, operating in it would work like clockwork. The ingredients of faith are to speak, think and act.

Have you ever cooked a meal and left out one or two ingredients? Did it taste like the first time you ever tasted it? Did it turn out like the original recipe? Faith will not work if one or more of these ingredients are left out. Speaking, thinking, and acting are vital for our faith to work and get the desired results of what the Word declares.

Faith comes by hearing and hearing by the Word of God. To hear, we have to speak or say exactly what the Word of God says about us. How do we have faith in God? Jesus said, "Whosoever shall say unto this mountain, be thou removed and be though cast into the sea and shall not doubt in his heart, but shall believe (in his heart) that those things which he saith shall come to pass, he shall have whatsoever he saith" (Mark 11:23, parentheses added).

Three times Jesus referred to our saying, speaking, declaring, or commanding. So for us to have faith in God, we must say what he has already said. Proverbs 18:21 tells us, "Death and life are in the power of the tongue." We have spent most of our time saying what others have said about us or the lies of the devil.

We have spoken things about and over ourselves that have kept us in bondage to words of death and not words of life. This is why it is hard for us to hear positive things spoken to us. We can change that; it's not that we can't believe in positive things, but our emotions and thoughts are not accustomed to those things. As we stay with the Word of God, they will line up with the truth.

There is nothing wrong with us. We must discipline ourselves to say what God says, and in time our emotions and thoughts will come into agreement with his Word. What we speak by faith will change the state of our heart so that it again serves our spirit. Now we can see what the devil is afraid of; he knows that once we view ourselves as God says we are, our confidence will soar, and we will not bow to the lies and strategies he wages against us.

Jesus lived this way. In John 8:26, Jesus said, "And I speak to the world those things which I have heard of him." In verse 28, he says, "But as my Father hath taught me, I speak these things," and in verse 29, he adds, "And he that sent me is with me: the Father hath not left me alone; for I do always those things that please him."

In Hebrews 11:6, we read, "But without faith it is impossible to please him: for he that cometh to God must believe that he is, and that he is a rewarder of them that diligently seek him." Faith pleases God. Faith is for the spiritual realities God has provided. Notice that the focus of faith is to be on what God has said. Jesus did not come up with anything to say; he set his will on pleasing his Father by repeating what he knew his Father had said to him.

We have the Bible to tell us what Father God said so that we can repeat it as Jesus did, and we will obtain the same results in our life as he did in his. Speaking is an ingredient of faith. We have spoken perverted faith—also known as fear—all of our life, but now as children of God, it's time to speak life to and over ourselves, viewing ourselves as we are in Christ. As with Jesus, so is it to be with us. We are to view ourselves as God declared concerning us.

Living by faith removes us from the cursed life of the first Adam and re-establishes our heart in the reality of the last Adam, where we are blessed. We are a spirit, our heart and soul are spiritual, and faith is for our heart and soul, so the truth of God can abide there. God would not save us and let our heart, soul, and mind stay in a state at odds with our spirit.

We are to believe by confessing the Word of God; he will take our act of faith and rebuild within our heart his view. We must begin using our mouth to declare what God has declared so that we can see ourselves rightly. The next ingredient for faith to work is our thought life. Our thoughts—what we think about ourselves—have to agree with what we say, and what we say must agree with the Word for it to be faith. Faith not only speaks; it also thinks.

We must develop "faith thoughts" about ourselves. To do this, we must have a pure, righteous, godly faith view of ourselves. We don't think in words; we think in pictures. If I say to you, "Describe an apple," you would describe the image of the apple that you see within yourself and use words to convey the image of that apple.

We think in picture form and express the views we have of ourselves with our words, thoughts, and actions. Romans 12 says for us not to be conformed to this world but to be transformed by the renewing of our minds that we may prove what is the good, acceptable, and perfect will of God. Notice that we are not to remain conformed in our thinking to the way the world taught us to think.

Remember, in Ephesians 4, we are told to be renewed in the spirit of our mind and to "put on the new man," who after God is created in righteousness and true holiness. Our mind, our thought life, the images, and the pictures inside of our heart are to be renewed from flesh to being a spirit, for we are alive unto God and carry the name of God's Son, in whom he is well pleased. Our thinking is to be transformed and renewed to the truth of the Word of God.

I had the speaking part down, but it did not start working for me until I started thinking in agreement with the Word I was speaking to myself, and then an explosion took place in my heart and I began to see myself the way God said he sees me in Christ. He brought me to this truth in Joshua 1:8, where he says, "This book of the law shall not depart out of your mouth; but you shall meditate therein day and night, that thou mayest observe to do according to all that is written therein: for then thou shalt make thy way prosperous, and then thou shalt have good success."

The book of the law is the Word of God; it is his book of our covenant, kingdom, and legal rights with him. The next truth we are told is that his word is to be in our mouths; we are to be saying and confessing what is legally ours. It's not wrong for us to say what God already said. This is what Jesus did, and it worked for him flawlessly. The next thing we are told to do is meditate, which means to think and meditate on—not just now and then but "day and night."

We understand that we can't think on the word literally all day and all night because there are other things in our life that we must give thought to, but at every opportunity we have to think, we are to return to thinking in agreement with his Word, without deviating from it for any reason. Our focus is to please Father God with the faith we are giving him, so don't worry about others and what they think. Remain true to viewing yourself by faith.

Thinking is vital to our faith working at its highest potential. We understand that it's based on what God said about us and not on what we've done, where we've missed it, or what others have said. As our views of ourselves change, it will be like being born again. It's the life and nature of God taking hold in our heart.

So far, we have seen two of the three ingredients of faith: the first is saying, the second is thinking, and the third is doing or acting in agreement with the will of God. Using Joshua 1:8, the next discipline is for us to observe to do according to all that is written therein. Doing is vital to faith's operation. Faith is never still; it is always working and moving toward the fulfillment of the Word of God.

We all have seen a cake baked or some type of food prepared, but what good would it do to combine all the ingredients and never put it in the oven or on the stove to cook it? It would not be something we could consume. If we say and think in line with the Word but never set out to act like it is true, we will never experience the reality of the Word.

In James, we are told to be doers of the word, not hearers only deceiving our own selves. In meditating on this verse, I asked the

Lord, "How will I know what to do?" His response caused me to look more intently at his word. I had focused on doing as I was trained, but the answer is observing to do. The answer is seeing myself doing it in my heart before doing it naturally. Many times, we strike out to do what the Word says without the faith view of it in our heart.

With some things, there is nothing we can physically do, but we can carry ourselves like we are what he says we are, picturing or viewing in our minds how to conduct ourselves in any given situation. For example, what can we do to show we are loved? Not much, but we can picture the response we have because we are loved.

We can develop the faith view of a loved person and interact with others accordingly. I pictured myself responding in a loving attitude, as a son of God, toward others, and when I was around people, I was not defensive, scared, or withdrawn. I was open, free, and looking to be a blessing. The love reality was acted out in my heart, and the whole environment changed.

We are faith children of the faith God, and we are to develop the view of ourselves that is based on faith. We do this by mixing the three ingredients of faith (speaking, thinking, and doing) together in our heart and then watching the Spirit of God go to work on changing the state of our heart into that of having heaven on earth.

What is the end result of mixing these ingredients of faith together? We will have good success and be prosperous in life from the inside out. Child of God, begin developing God's view of you in your heart. Develop the faith view inside yourself of how God sees you, and you will have success and prosper in life like Jesus did. Resist the old ways of speaking, thinking, and acting. Cast them down, give them no place in your life, and let God's will be your focus.

Don't get ahead of God and go for a Goliath like I did, when I could not handle Mr. Ant. Start out where you are and build the faith view in your heart from there because the abundant life is yours. Know this: God is pleased when we allow him to transform our life into his reality in the face of the devil who works to get us to believe that there is nothing God can do to change our situation.

But the devil is wrong. God not only can but he already did, through the cross of Christ. And the Spirit of God is here to manifest this reality in our life. Declare this: "I give the Holy Spirit the faith he needs to change the view of my life into the view of being and living as a child of God."

Chapter 11

Conclusion

In conclusion, the way we were raised spiritually to see ourselves is not the standard God established for us. God gave us life where he is the focus; he did not make us to be dependent upon things. Our life flows from the inner, spiritual view residing in our heart. God established the image and likeness for man to govern his life according to. At the point when man died spiritually, his view of himself changed into a perverted view of what God set him out to be.

From the fall of the first Adam to the resurrection of the last, man was bound to an inner image of himself, in which he could never see or live above being flesh. The Word calls this view being fleshly or carnally minded. This truth means that one can be a Christian spiritually yet still be fleshly or carnally minded at heart. With this understanding, there is nothing wrong with us; we are in the process of having our heart, soul, and mind—our control center—saved.

Our enemy desires for us to challenge our position. He wants us to doubt our salvation, the blood of Jesus, believing that nothing about us has or can change. We learned to believe things about ourselves based on what we do and not on who we are. Under the New Covenant, God placed his judgment, which we deserved, upon Jesus, his Son.

Let's look at an Old Covenant reference to Jesus before we look at a shorter New Testament version. Isaiah 53:1–12 says,

Who hath believed our report? and to whom is the arm of the LORD revealed? For he shall grow up before him as a tender plant, and as a root out of a dry ground: he hath no form nor comeliness; and when we shall see him, there is no beauty that we should desire him. He is despised and rejected of men; a man of sorrows, and acquainted with grief: and we hid as it were our faces from him; he was despised, and we esteemed him not. Surely he hath borne our griefs, and carried our sorrows: yet we did esteem him stricken, smitten of God, and afflicted. But he was wounded for our transgressions, he was bruised for our iniquities: the chastisement of our peace was upon him; and with his stripes we are healed. All we like sheep have gone astray; we have turned every one to his own way; and the LORD hath laid on him the iniquity of us all. He was oppressed, and he was afflicted, yet he opened not his mouth: he is brought as a lamb to the slaughter, and as a sheep before her shearers is dumb, so he openeth not his mouth. He was taken from prison and from judgment: and who shall declare his generation? for he was cut off out of the land of the living: for the transgression of my people was he stricken. And he made his grave with the wicked, and with the rich in his death; because he had done no violence, neither was any deceit in his mouth. Yet it pleased the LORD to bruise him; he hath put him to grief: when thou shalt make his soul an offering for sin, he shall see his seed, he shall prolong his days, and the pleasure of the LORD shall prosper in his hand. He shall see of the travail of his soul, and shall be satisfied: by his knowledge shall my righteous servant justify many; for he shall bear their iniquities. Therefore will I divide him a portion with the great, and he shall divide the spoil with the strong; because he hath poured out his soul unto death: and he was numbered with the transgressors; and he bare the sin of many, and made intercession for the transgressors.

Man faced judgment spirit, soul, and body, but God put it all on Jesus. And he took it to the cross and then to the grave, but when he arose from the dead, judgment stayed and he was set free. What God has done for us far outweighed the sin in our life. Because of Jesus, we have the right to be free in our heart from the perverted view we inherited from the first Adam and to re-establish the perfect view of the last Adam.

The New Testament version of this verse is found in 2 Corinthians 5:21, which states, "For he hath made him to be sin for us, who knew no sin; that we might be made the righteousness of God in him." By the blood of Jesus, we have been made the righteousness of God in him, which is Christ; it is a must for the view of ourselves to be changed into the righteous view of who we are in Christ.

This righteous view is the view God has maintained for us even after man had turned his back on him. He longed for the day when he would set man free from the selfish judgment of the first Adam, making available the right to be made anew—first in our spirit, then our soul, and last our physical body.

God made the provision for all humanity to be born out of the sin nature and made righteous before him again. The Word calls this provision being saved or born again. However, this is just the beginning, not the end. Now is the time for salvation; today is it. Once we receive Jesus as our Savior and Lord, we are positioned to begin the new journey of having our heart, soul, mind, or control center saved, making them compatible with our spirit.

James 1:21 says, "Wherefore lay apart all filthiness and superfluity of naughtiness, and receive with meekness the engrafted word, which is able to save your souls." God desires for our control center to be restored to righteousness as he has made our spirit. Herein is where religion has let us down. Faith to the religious is based on their denomination and its beliefs, not on the finished work of Christ.

Our struggle is in our control center, where the perverted view of ourselves resides. It's not the changing of the view that's hard; rather it's the changing of the feelings and emotions that proves difficult. Our feelings and emotions are supporters of our spirit. We learned to let them lead us in everything about our life. We attached our feelings and emotions to everything, and now here comes God telling us to return to living life by faith, which requires us to stop depending on them for direction.

Be encouraged. We can change the view of ourselves into the view God has for us. We have to resist letting our understanding from our experiences blind us to things existing outside of it, like those in the "One Size Fits All" story.

His truth requires a change in the view or image, in our heart. Stay with the Word and meditate on what he says, giving the Holy Spirit the right to change the view from being perverted back to the perfect view of being just like Jesus, and we will see that he has truly blessed us with all spiritual blessings in Christ.

Notes

Chapter 1

[1] *Webster's Revised Unabridged 1913 Edition Dictionary,* available from http://www.webster-dictionary.org/definition/view, s.v., "view."

[2] *Webster's New World College Dictionary,* 4th ed., available from http://www.yourdictionary.com/conception, s.v., "conception"

[3] *Merriam-Webster Dictionary,* since 1828, available from https://www.merriam-webster.com/dictionary/peer%20pressure, s.v., "peer pressure"

Chapter 2

[1] *Webster's New World College Dictionary,* 4th ed., available from http://www.yourdictionary.com/conception, s.v., "conditional"

[2] Ibid

Chapter 3

[1] *Webster's New World College Dictionary,* 4th ed., available from http://www.yourdictionary.com/conception, s.v., "perfect"

Chapter 5

[1] James Strong, *Strong's Exhaustive Concordance of the Bible,* "Greek and Hebrew Dictionary", s.v., "glass" 2 Corinthians 3:18

Chapter 6

1 *Webster's New World College Dictionary*, 4th ed., available from http://www.yourdictionary.com/conception, s.v., "hybrid"
2 Ibid

Chapter 7

1 *Webster's New World College Dictionary*, 4th ed., available from http://www.yourdictionary.com/citizen, s.v., "citizen"
2 *Online Etymology Dictionary*, http://www.etymonline.com/index.php?term=treason, s.v., "treason"
3 Vine, W. E., Merrill F. Unger, William White, and W. E. Vine. 1985. *Vine's complete expository dictionary of Old and New Testament words*. Nashville: Nelson., s.v., "commonwealth"

Chapter 8

1 *Webster's Revised Unabridged 1913 Edition Dictionary*, available from http://www.webster-dictionary.org/definition/view, s.v., "constitution."
2 James Strong, *Strong's Exhaustive Concordance of the Bible*, "Greek and Hebrew Dictionary", s.v., "government"
3 *Online Etymology Dictionary*, http://www.etymonline.com/index.php?term=government, s.v., "government"

Chapter 9

1 *Online Etymology Dictionary*, http://www.etymonline.com/index.php?term=imagination, s.v., "imagination".

Printed in the United States
By Bookmasters